Help! I'm Going CRAZY!

By Terri Ann Laws

Westlands House Publishing

For my children, Daniel, Nathan and Seth

And

In loving memory of Guy Flemmer. You are a beautiful soul and we will always remember you.

First edition published by : **Westlands House Publishing**

A catalogue record of this book is available from the British library

ISBN of this edition – 978-0-9556231-0-3

Art and cover design - Alex Penderis
Final layout and preparation - Graeme Gets
Distributed by Pondering Fool Ltd

Cartoon drawings in the book – Alex Penderis and Karen Laing

First edition published in 2008

Printed and bound in the UK by CPI Mackays, Chatham ME5 8TD

Contents

Foreword

This is a well written book written by a truly remarkable women. Her courage in the face of seemingly impossible circumstances is proof the ultimate power of mind and spirit over matter. It is a testimony to one women's extraordinary ingenuity and creativity to not only survive but thrive under conditions where most would have given up. Terri Ann was forced to live on the streets of South Africa with her young children while she was constantly on the run from a vindictive and violent husband. For her and her children to survive on the street required coping skills and an unbelievable positive mental attitude.

This is the path of her learning and return back to sanity. Terri Ann read several hundred books on modern thinking and psychology, carefully reading and summarizing each book to extract the learnings and weighed them up against impossible living conditions. This is the real magic of this book. Most writers make one or two main points and base their book on that. Few ever test their ideas against real world conditions. In this amazing text Terri Ann summarizes the lessons from literally hundreds of books and demonstrates how to actually apply these ideas, even under the most harrowing of circumstances. Above all it is full of practical advice showing each of us how to find and maintain our own sanity.

'Help! I'm Going Crazy!' will benefit anyone who wants to understand how to survive and thrive in real life. It is about ideas and even more important it is about applications. It is written with a mixture of humour and seriousness and sprinkled with Terri Ann's amazing poetry which is both apt and amusing. I encourage everyone to read and benefit from this book. It is a comprehensive summary of modern ideas and a real example of how they can actually be applied in the circumstances of everyday living. It is easy to read and immediately applicable to coping with all of the circumstances and challenges of life.

Amazingly Terri Ann survived and her children are grown now. She has gone on to become an international master trainer, a healer, a therapist, a life skills coach, a business women, a presenter and a writer devoted to helping others find the happiness and sanity she found. This is a real guide written from the heart and it will touch your heart, mind and spirit. It is the ultimate user's guide for living, coping and thriving in today's dysfunctional world. Everybody should read it, and not just those who have more problems than they know how to deal with. Each page contains eye opening flashes of the blindingly obvious which make you wonder how you didn't see the way yourself. Every chapter is helpful and you will probably read it over and over again. It is the kind of book that you can't put down and that you want to share with friends and relatives.

Wyatt L. Woodsmall, Ph.D.

NLP Master Trainer and Master Modeler. Co-founder of Time Line Therapy, co-founder of INLPTA and writer of several books including 'People Pattern Power' and co-author of 'Time Line Therapy and the Basis of Personality'.

A Word About Me

I don't imagine there are too many people who messed up their lives quite as badly as I did, who made quite as many mistakes, wrong turns, errors of judgement, bad choices and horrible life situations. I could blame it on a traumatic, abusive childhood or on a traumatic, abusive marriage or on my mental condition at the time. I could blame the failings of society or the nuns at the convent where I went to school. I could blame any number of things, and all of those things would excuse me absolutely in the eyes and opinions of the general public. In fact, I could get a tremendous amount of sympathy. All the consequences to others could be not my fault given my reasons. I could have become a burden on the state and checked into a safe mental home for good and let someone else bring up my kids and bail me out. I decided instead to take responsibility and fix up my life. I decided to put myself in the driver's seat and find out what works and what doesn't work, and learn to recognise the signs and understand what makes the difference. I reasoned that if some people can live a wonderful, happy life while others exist in a living hell, then there is probably some kind of art, some set of skills, some way of being in the world or some kind of knowledge, that some have and others lack. I decided to find out what made successful happy people that way, and discover how I could make that happen for me. I was at a crisis point and I had to make a choice – check out or check in.

What's the Book About?

So many things in life drive us crazy. Traffic, work, demands, kids, our partners, bad relationships, queues, arguments, frustrations, misunderstandings, expectations, bad service, things that don't work, equipment that fails, debt, rip-off artists, to name but a few. And then there is just life in general and trying to make sense of it. Why do other people behave and react as they do? Why don't things turn out or work as they should? What's the matter with everyone?

In this stressful life we all live these days, so many things make everything worse - but the root cause of it all is, believe it or not, inside ourselves. It's inner conflict. The less we are able to predict, shape and control our lives, the worse things get. The worse things get, the less we are able to cope. The less we cope, the more things go wrong, the more we lose our grip - until we feel that we are going absolutely crazy.

This guide is basically the learning path that I took myself through. It is my belief and hope that it will take you from a hectic, mad, rushed, frantic - or confused, frustrated, helpless space into a calm position of strength, peace, control and understanding. We can gain a lot more control over our lives and over the things that happen to us. Empowerment and personal leadership should be deliberate choices that we make, but for most people, a few things need to change in us before we are really able to make those choices.

The lessons in this book will teach you skills and techniques and give you tools to help with a number of important things such as coping with inner conflict, combating guilt and fear, and relating more effectively and successfully with others. You will learn to make sense of a lot of things that happen, and to cope more easily with all the things that might normally drive you crazy. It will teach you how to create for yourself a much happier and more peaceful life.

It's not meant to be the kind of book you just read once. You can, and probably should, keep referring to it because it has so much in it on so many levels. The concepts, wisdom and revelations are collected from a wide range of sources, so you could see it as a kind of textbook. Each chapter stands alone and can be read on its own. You can read the bits you feel you need without having to read any other part of the book first.

Twelve years of intensive study, research and practical application has gone into this collection of applicable wisdom from various sources. I feel confident you can completely trust every word in it as sound, sensible, usable, workable advice because it was gleaned from the works and writings of the very best gurus, mentors and personal growth specialists of our time. I then tested it on the many clients and students I have helped through teaching and counselling. You may recognize bits and pieces from many great authors everywhere. It is the lazy way to read one hundred books. I read and studied at least four hundreds books, and found profound wisdom in about twenty-five per cent of them. This book is the result of my studies, and my conclusions.

I've also attended dozens of personal growth courses, professional development courses and seminars, gained a lot of professional qualifications in the field and bought hundreds of home-study packs of CDs, videos, DVDs, and tapes and studied them in fine detail. I learned how to help people become functional, successful and happy, and of course, I learned how to be that way myself. I made a career out of personal growth and development, and I've helped thousands of people to create the life they want.

So many times in life we don't see the wood for the trees, and we push the lifeboat to one side because it is blocking our way and our view of the shore we are so desperately trying to swim towards. It is my hope and belief that this book will illuminate the lifeboat for you and give you a set of paddles as well.

Help! I'm Going Crazy!

I want to go crazy, lose my head
And fall off the wall completely
I need an excuse to give up on life
And get away with it so sweetly.

I want to become incapable
And disregard all of my duties.
And any behaviour I choose to display
Could be blamed on my new set of muties*

Then I'd be free to play all day
Drawing and singing and painting.
If anyone told me to do anything
I'd just begin shaking and fainting.

by Terri Ann Laws

(* muties – African word meaning medicines)

The Scots poet Robert Burns wrote;

"Would to God the grace he gie us To see ourselves as others see us."

All ancient wisdom, religions and philosophy tell us in different ways to 'know ourselves'. Most famous autobiographies include 'self discovery', when the person (hero) did things they never knew were in them to do. Look at all the people around you and say to yourself: "What do you see when you see me?" Chances are you don't know the answer to that question. You can only guess and hope you are right. We can't really know who we are until we make the effort to find out.

When you really know yourself, you never feel unfamiliar or awkward. You never worry about who, how or what you are to yourself or to other people. You can trust yourself to do, to be and to say all the right things in almost any situation. The more you get to know yourself, the more you get to like yourself, and the more you get to like yourself, the more you're able to relax and be yourself. And, oddly enough, the more you like yourself, the more you tend to like others, and that makes you an altogether more likeable person.

So how do we get to know ourselves really well?
This is a very slow process for two reasons. The first is because we are so complex and we have thousands of facets. The second is because we have to develop a huge amount of courage before we can even consider, let alone openly admit, that some of our habits or traits are distinctly bad. We are desperate to see ourselves, and have others see

2

us, as good: good company, good character, good provider, good parent, good worker, good friend etc.

In important circumstances we try to be what we feel others expect us to be, so we feel we have to put on an act and be politically correct or polite or something else. This acting can make us feel drained and insecure because we are never quite sure if we handled the situation well, made a good impression or behaved correctly. We often replay the scenario to ourselves afterwards a few times over to judge ourselves. If we decide we did well we feel happy, and if we decide we did badly we feel terrible.

This analysis is not always constructive. When it is not constructive, it does not help us to grow and learn, but is more likely to teach us to be even more careful, suspicious, closed and self conscious, which is very bad for us. We want to be free, relaxed, open and confident in every situation and with all people. We want to 'be ourselves' at all times, hence the phrase 'I can't be myself with him/her/them,' implying that some situations and some people make us feel ill at ease or uncomfortable.

Actually there is no 'real me' inside me and no 'real you' inside you. There is no fixed, unchangeable, permanent person over whom we have no control, who just happens to feel different ways in different situations or company. We limit ourselves terribly if we subscribe to the theory that we are what we are and that's that. This theory is quite untrue. We can change drastically and instantly as a result of some major experience. If you were to change religions, many things in you would change. When you are first promoted to a position of authority, many things in you change. If war broke out and the city closed down, many things in you would change. We can also choose to change for our own personal reasons.

To use a computer metaphor (since computers are fashioned after the human brain), we are programmed with many programs. We have different software applications loaded. If we find we have the software to handle a situation we find ourselves in, we feel comfortable. We know exactly what to do without even having to think about it, and we do it spontaneously and unconsciously and things flow. We don't become tense, we don't feel we have to act and we don't worry about it afterwards. If fact we feel good. We always feel good when our intercommunications go well and when things run smoothly. But when the opposite happens, it's only because we are not sure of our programming or we lack certain packages of software, and then everything seems to be difficult, strained or awkward and just don't work right.

If you got to know your computer really well you would be able to use it quickly and efficiently for any task you wanted it to perform. You would also know when it was time to change the programming or add new software or perhaps even upgrade the whole computer. You could also detect a virus or system failure straight away.

We can change our programming: our ideas, our convictions, in fact anything about our character and personality. We are not fixed, unchangeable beings, we are beings in process. At any given time we are only, as J Powell put it, what we:

| think | judge | feel |
| value | honour | esteem |

| love | hate | fear |
| desire | hope | believe |

and are committed to.

All of these fluctuate. They come into us through our senses (eyes, ears, feelings, etc.) at some time or other during our lifetimes. None of them were there when we were born and every one of them can be changed if we choose to change them.

If I'd been raised from birth with the blacks in darkest Africa I would have grown up to love sour milk and mielie meal. However, I was not and I hate those foods. If I'd been raised a Hindu in India I would feel offended at the mention of beef. However I was not and I am happy to cook steak for my partner. I do not feel as though I am committing a sin when I buy it or if I were to eat it.

Other people have put all our programming into our heads, and we have probably put a lot of programming into other people's heads as well. Every time you convince someone of anything you change their programming a tiny little bit. We are constantly giving out and taking in data. We are always trying to have an effect on each other and share information and have people accept what we say.

But we are not victims of our programming. Your machine computer can do nothing to defend itself when you insert a disk, or program the hard drive. But we are human. We are able to protect ourselves. We can hear, see and feel and choose not to be affected by it. We can say, "I hear what you are saying and it is interesting. Thank you for sharing that with me, and it is OK with me for you to believe that, but I prefer to hold on to my own opinion." In other

5

words, I choose not to be influenced/programmed. I make my own decisions and choices, and I pick my own software and programming.

We are constantly hearing, seeing and reading things. We think, formulate and imagine things all the time too. These are all input. It is not what input we receive that is important, but what we do with it once we have received it. There are many things we could do with input, for example:

- Remember and use later.
- Judge it rubbish and throw it in the recycle bin.
- Save! Add to programming or replace programming and apply.
- Add to a software package and use in certain applications only.
- Confusion! Add to files pending and deal with later.
- View as serious infringement! Attack, defend, react, do something, do not ignore.

And you could think of dozens of other responses. To look at one example, if someone were to tell you a dirty joke that was in bad taste but yet actually was very funny, you would scan your programming quickly and decide which software package to load. Perhaps you loaded the one called 'be appropriate' or 'religious conviction', or 'God', or 'I am proper'. Then you might squash your urge to laugh and choose your distaste response. Or you could perhaps load one called 'I am fun', give in to your urge to laugh and enjoy a chuckle. We can't not respond in some way. It is important though to be aware of the fact that on some level we respond to all input even when we pretend not to or try not to respond. Becoming more aware of that helps us to take responsibility for our own responses and choices and programming and their consequences.

Whichever choice you made on the spot about the joke, you will still have to do something with that input.

You might remember the joke and repeat it only when it seemed safe to do so.

You would be very unlikely to update your view of the world over it, because a joke is hardly the sort of thing you would change your life over.

If you are a religious person and still chose to enjoy a chuckle, you might feel bad about it and consider updating your choices for future reference. When you make a choice that conflicts with your values, it *does* affect your programming and could cause a virus, because the two might not live together in peace.

You may think of many different things you could do with the various input you receive. We are all individual. There are thousands of choices and variations, each with their own set of cause and effects and consequences.

So many of our reactions and responses are automatic, flowing unconsciously and spontaneously from our deeply imbedded habits, and can be hard to recognise and even harder to change. Singling them out and examining them one by one is a slow and deliberate process, but a journey more worthwhile than you could ever imagine. Let's begin with an obviously bad one, such as something we do or some response we don't like about ourselves, something we want to change, some reaction that others have told us is not our highest and best.

Try making a list of all the things that make you angry. You can examine the list and ask yourself why you allow those things to make you angry. Then think of some people you know who would not be angered by those things. Again, reflect on why that is and what the differences are between them and you. Then can begin writing yourself a new program, deciding how you would rather behave and feel in future when faced with those things that used to make you angry. When you've got it all sorted out, apply the new program and practise your new response till it flows automatically.

It takes some practice at first, but the more you do it the better you get at it, and the benefits are compounded because you also get practice at the practice of making changes and upgrades to yourself, so future changes become progressively easier to make.

It is like learning to drive a car. When you first learn you are painfully aware of all the pedals, the gears, the indicators and everything. You concentrate on your coordination and the road all at the same time. After much practice, everything you need to do becomes automatic and you don't have to think about it anymore. Then you can hold a conversation or make a business call on your phone while driving in heavy traffic perfectly safely.

Imagine now that they brought out a new type of car that had foot steering and fifteen computerised buttons operated from a keyboard by your fingers for driving! Driving would no longer be automatic to you anymore. You would have to learn how to drive all over again, concentrating hard when first you took your new car into the traffic. But before long, you would have adapted. If you see changes as a hassle, they are harder to make. If you see changes as a challenge, especially if you see them as a fun challenge, they are easier to make. Attitude makes a big difference, especially in the area of motivation.

The bad programs in us will be all the ones that cause us to feel uncomfortable, such as angry, hurt, stressed, panic, depressed, or any way we don't like feeling. Bad programs are also those programs that get us to speak and behave in ways we don't like to speak and behave. The good programs in us usually outweigh, and are far more numerous, than the bad ones. These good ones are the ones that prompt us to laugh, help people, behave competently, protect, nurture, make decisions, learn new skills, discern between right and wrong, apologise... I could fill a page with examples. So ultimately, we are not really bad us humans. We are generally good, and we have the capacity to be even better. In fact we owe it to ourselves for the sake of our happiness to make the effort.

It is very important to realize here that nobody can make us angry or hurt or anything else for that matter. It is our programming that decides which words or deeds should trigger which response. We are conditioned to react or behave in a certain way according to a certain stimulus, and we can change our conditioning, our minds, our automatic responses and reactions, and we can change our programming. *We are never helpless victims of our programming.*

Emotional responses we suddenly find ourselves enveloped in are actually a product of our expectations, not our conditions. Our expectations are the things that hurt and frustrate us. If you expect a loved one to treat you in a certain way and they don't, they have not failed you, they have failed your expectations. If you were to change the expectation, you wouldn't feel that way anymore. If someone makes you angry, it is because you expected them to behave or speak in a certain way, and they did not. They behaved and spoke in a way you disapprove of, a way that was contrary to your expectations. Therefore it is not they who have made you angry but your expectations. If you changed the expectation, you wouldn't get angry with that person anymore.

We often don't realise that it is actually unreasonable to expect other people to choose their words or actions for our comfort and convenience, or to match our rules and norms, and yet at the same time, we don't like it when others expect the same of us. Many relationships break up because each person makes up a long list of arbitrary expectations of the other and then demands these expectations be lived up to. Each appoints themselves as judge over the other based on these expectations, keeping score and using 'failures' as ammunition, and blaming the others' 'sins' for all the fighting or unhappiness between them. Each one expects the other to change, and to accept them as they are, neither one realising the contradiction in terms!

Because of our own perspective and our own self-protective instincts, we are all very good at twisting things to make it sound like the other person is guilty of some unforgivable offence when we feel offended. We seldom think to question the feeling itself to see if it is valid or fair to feel that way. We think it is obvious if we feel bad, that it must be somebody's fault. Well, this is true, but the somebody is usually ourselves - our understanding, expectations and assumptions.

So tell me who of us is bad,
Since we all think we're good.
We know the reasons why we do,
What we think we should.

Yet many deeds when cleanly stripped
Of all their reasons why,
Are wicked things within themselves
Yet to ourselves we lie.

I've never met a human yet,
Who honestly agrees
That what he chose to do was bad,
Unless he's on his knees.

By Terri Ann Laws

We usually have two reasons for doing things: the noble reason and the truth. The noble reasons are those carefully thought out ones that we feel are acceptable and are a better way to explain it to others. The other reason is the truth. Unless we have a good, close friend or mentor whom we can really trust to stand by us and believe in us no matter what we say or do or confess to, we can sometimes not really face or get to the truth of most matters. Some things are just too scary to look at. Here's a prize example just to entertain you:

I need to be sickly, frail and in pain
So people can see how I suffer.,
Then when I cope in spite of it all,
I need them to say I am tougher.

I often must mention the troubles I have.
It's really important they know it.
So they can see that it's harder for me,
I need to make sure that I show it.

by Terri Ann Laws

Because of our self-protect mechanisms, we all have a lot of trouble admitting that sort of stuff and are far more likely to have some good noble reasons for the way we are. A lady told me, after she'd read my poem, that she would never have been able to admit to such a thing a few years earlier, but now she was able to laugh at herself. There are people who are always the victims of villains, people who always have huge amounts of endless bad luck, people who feel other people don't give them the respect they deserve, and people who have one failed relationship after another. Sometimes we don't even realize a negative habit or problem exists, and we feel very offended or defensive if someone notices it or makes a comment.

However, we can make huge progress in a lot of areas of our lives and get to know quite a considerable amount of ourselves, all by ourselves, with the help of books. Some of my favourite authors are Steven Covey, Erick Fromm, Wayne Dyer, John Powell and anything on the subject of Neuro-linguistic Programming (NLP). There are hundreds of authors and titles to choose from in the book stores and the library and you are bound to find a few writers who appeal to you particularly. But you know, books won't help you at all unless you first learn how to read them properly.

People read these 'human condition' books on one of four levels:

1. **The search for what I need to hear**

    If you are reading on this level, you will be scanning dozens of books in search of statements that will clarify what you already believe to be true. Your filters will be those of self-justification, self-validation and proof for self. In this case, 90% of all the material in the books will fly right by you, wasted, because you will discount, ignore or disagree with everything that does not fit your existing picture.

2. **Everyone else is also**

    If you are reading on this level you will be recognizing yourself in a lot of places, but instead of using this information to understand yourself better, you will be using it to understand human kind better. You will be comforting yourself with the fact that lots of people also have the same problems you have, and you will feel no need to change or grow since it is 'normal'. This kind of reading might make you a great counsellor, psychologist or mentor for others, but it will do little to make you happy or help you fix your own life.

3. **Spot the Baddie**

    This is vindictive reading. If you are reading on this level, what you will be doing is entertaining yourself by recognizing other people you know. While you are reading, your thoughts might go something like this:

15

"Hah! That describes Joe Soap to a T!"

"Oh My mother should read this. This'll put her straight."

"So this is what's wrong with my husband/wife!"

"I think I should give my neighbour a copy of this chapter."

And on you go through the books. Again you waste 90% of all the material you read because you're only finding faults in others and others are not likely to want you to change them. For the information to be useful to you, you need to be willing to consider that the material may well apply to you personally.

4. **Help! I'm going crazy!**

If you are reading on this level you will be realizing that something is wrong in your life and you are determined to fix it, and you will also be realizing that it is entirely up to you to change things. You will be reading with an open mind and a strong desire to pay careful attention; to grow, to learn, to expand your comfort zones and to find solutions to your problems. You apply everything you read to yourself only, since it is yourself you are trying to heal or help. This is 100% constructive and you will enjoy a wealth of benefits even after the very first book.

Those reading on levels 1, 2 or 3 are also doing so to fix their lives, but they think they need to find out what's wrong with everyone else. They hope to find a way to fix the problem by putting others right.

The more we read and apply material, the more we get to know ourselves. The better we know ourselves, the better equipped we are to examine our programming and software. The more we examine our programming and software, the more we will understand it (ourselves) and the more efficiently and effectively we can use it (to function well in the world), and the easier it is to see what needs changing. All kinds of bad memories, hurts, disappointments, bitterness, ongoing perpetrating problems, and unresolved issues can be healed instantly sometimes just by seeing things differently, by understanding on a different level.

As we read we learn, as we learn we grow, as we apply what we learn we grow in quantum leaps. We grow until we are bigger than the problem that seemed so much bigger than us at first. Once we are bigger than the problem, it becomes so easy to solve it. Einstein said, 'We cannot solve our problems at the same level of thinking we were at when we created them.'

A five year old went into the local café with his own money to buy his own sweets all by himself for the first time one day. Waiting in the car were his two brothers and his mother. He stopped at the door and looked back for encouragement. "Go on, you can do it! It's nothing", encouraged one brother, sweeping the air with hands. The other brother laughed and said, "He'll never do it, he's too chicken."

The mother scolded both boys saying, "Oh stop it!", and watched the little one to see if he'd succeed.

The little boy felt terrified and under great pressure. The world had given him a task to see if he was good enough, if he could cut it, so to speak. He walked into the shop trying to look as confident as he could. As he got to the counter, he began to feel a bit panicky. He turned around to face the door. No, he couldn't chicken out, his one brother would mock him forever, and maybe tell everyone what a baby he is, and his Mum might not trust him with 'big' things again. He remembered the encouragement of his other brother and tried to draw strength from it. He looked at the big, scary, impatient shopkeeper. He looked at all the many varieties of sweets and he wished he knew how many, or which sweets he could buy with his money. He simply had to do this, but it was so traumatic for him.

I think we can all relate to the above metaphor. Panic is one result of expecting huge amounts from ourselves without taking the time to properly grow into the new, bigger shoes we've decided to wear, or feel we have to wear. We just expect ourselves to know or to be able. We stand halfway between metaphorical shopkeepers and doorways and 'imagine' the worst that can happen. We imagine consequences that are often way out of proportion to reality. All we need to do to grow way too big for the problems we face is to find out what in fact we are afraid of and why, what is it we need to work on, who we really are and what we are actually capable of. Then we can go out and learn anything we realize we don't know well enough yet.

That sounds so easy doesn't it? That's because it is. We have to be willing to put a little effort into growing ourselves, teaching ourselves, helping ourselves and stop expecting ourselves to know everything right up front. First we have to find out who exactly we are, and what are the specific parameters, skills and shortcomings of this package called a body-mind that we are wandering around this world in. If I think I already have all the answers, I'm doomed before I start. The more I think I know myself, the less enthusiastically I'll search. If I 'know' all the answers, then what have I to learn? People who think they 'know' are the very ones who stay stuck. We know a lot less than we think we do about who we really are inside. We are complex, fascinating, amazing mysteries, especially to ourselves.

Depression and Despondency, the two terrible 'D's, are nothing more than viruses. As we grow in self-realisation we find these terrible 'D's slowly dissolving. A good computer programmer never gets outsmarted by a virus. A virus is just a very clever piece of software sneaked in by a hacker into a place where it will cause damage or chaos. It is simply some hidden instructions set to be triggered by something. For example: '... at this point, delete common sense.' Or, 'When you have too much on your plate ... immediately get the urge to run away ...When you can't run away, immediately feel trapped.' Or, 'Don't let them get away with it! Lose your temper and make a big fuss!' Or, 'What's the point, what's the use, I might as well give up now'

The person we are is the person we have chosen to be. We didn't know until now that we were making choices. We didn't realise that we even had a choice. We have allowed all sorts of information to be loaded into our thinking, information that we have indiscriminately accepted, information that we have allowed to change us, programme us, alter our thinking, reasoning, feeling and actions. We've let the world shape us, but now that we know we are the ones doing the choosing, we need to take some serious action.

Who the hell am I and why am I here?
I'm constantly torn between laughter and fear.
I'm sometimes confused and often alone,
Aimlessly wandering further from home.

I don't want to be here, I don't want to leave,
My mind is changing, I dimly perceive.
I'm clutching on straws that just disappear,
Trying to maintain in this dim atmosphere.

Though I'm not able, I'm still holding on,
In case there's a future that's not yet gone.
Maybe the answer is simple and plain,
Perhaps it is that I don't know what I gain.

by Terri Ann Laws

Now that we know we are programmed and we are responsible for the programming, and the programming determines the quality of our entire lives, we must take immediate steps. We must take responsibility for our input and output. We must examine all the stuff that's already in us and decide what is good and what is bad, what must stay and what must go, what needs changing, rearranging or updating. For a start there are a lot of automatic reactions and feelings that need to be brought to heel. We can't allow rampant feelings to dictate the way we feel and behave all the time, can we?

A man went to visit a friend who had bought a new house. As they left the house in the morning, the friend greeted his neighbour with a big smile and a wave. The neighbour glanced up from his plants and scowled angrily, making a rude comment. The man, surprised, said to his friend,

"Gosh! Why is your neighbour so angry with you?"

"That's just the way he is. He's always like that" The friend explained.

"So do you always greet him so nicely?"

"Yes, every day."

"Why are you nice to him if he's always angry and rude to you?"

"Because I'm not going give up my happy mornings. I'm the happiest in the morning. I won't let that change now that I find myself with a miserable neighbour. His anger is his problem. I've no intention of becoming like him."

Obviously this person had decided not to allow or accept any negativity into his programming. He was not going to allow another man's problems to become his problems. He was not going to allow someone else's mood to decide what kind of mood or day he had. Bad vibes and bad attitudes are only contagious if we let them in.

How did the bad programming get in?

Every time we've felt any strong emotions, for instance irritated, hurt, rejected, misunderstood, frightened or angry, we've formulated for ourselves an opinion about it and a way to deal with it. We've accepted the input into our programming by allowing the input to change us in some way. By programming I mean our fundamental character. By software I mean applications like the things we chat about, our choice of people we would rather share a laugh with, and all the light, surface stuff that does not determine our deepest convictions or values. When the things that happen cause us to change as a person rather than just affecting us on the surface for the moment, I call that a change in programming.

These character changes turn us from being an open, innocent, gullible child into a cautious, defensive, reactive adult who sometimes feels he/she has to resort to acting, manipulating or just straight telling lies in order to survive. We have learned all kinds of defence mechanisms and retaliations. All these are bad programs that formed because we didn't know how to handle the powerful emotions we felt at the time. But as I said before, we do not have to remain a victim of any programming. Bad programs are like self-fulfilling prophecies. They distort our vision and make us miserable, so we ought to change them.

None of us wants to be a phoney, a fraud, two faced, insincere or plastic, and yet now and then we find ourselves in a situation where we feel compelled to behave in a very different manner from which we normally do. For example, it takes a tremendous amount of courage to speak out against the crowd when we don't like what they are saying. Yet we know that being there, a part of the group, in a way includes us in what they say, if we don't tell them that we disagree. Sometimes it isn't worth it, if there is nothing to gain and a lot to lose.

Imagine you are going for a job interview, and the pay is higher and the place is much closer to your home than your present place of employment. The job requirements are: 'Friendly person. Able to work under pressure.' Let's say you are an introverted, withdrawn person, and you usually stay quietly in the background. If you want the job, you behave in your friendliest and most open manner at the interview. Also, you know you get flustered under pressure but you want the job badly, so you tell the interviewer that you are fine with pressure. You don't deliberately lie. You first get all your noble reasons together.

You tell yourself, 'I can be friendly when I want to be,' and you prove this to yourself by being friendly at the interview. You say to yourself, 'I can work under pressure if I put my mind to it,' and you think of some occasion in your life when you have worked under pressure without becoming flustered. That's the difference between the noble reason and the truth. The truth is, you want to fool the interviewer into thinking that you are the person they advertised for, not because you could be if you tried, but because you want a better paying job closer to home. You can imagine this situation can't you? It's human nature, and it is what people do, then they wonder why they get problems.

Picture parents at home with their partners and kids, playing games and acting differently depending on what reaction or action they want to coerce out of others. We can change characters and become different, possibly all cute and coy if we think that is the best approach to get what we want, or we can turn into lawyers and argue our point with the genius of Einstein, or we can storm out, or storm in, and become a total pussy cat, or become a bulldog. When we are in a good mood we might say, 'No sweetie. Don't do that. Mummy/Daddy does not want you to do that.' Then when we are in a bad mood we might yell, at the top of our voice, 'If you ever do that again I'll slap you.' - same level of 'crime', very different reaction.

Usually when we blame our behaviour on our moods, we first ascribe the mood to being someone else's fault. We might say, 'The kids have been driving me crazy all day!' or 'They never listen until I shout and threaten.' Or 'That's the only thing that works with these people!' or "If they didn't do that then I wouldn't have to do this!" If I was to assume you caused my bad mood, then I would also assume you deserve the consequences I dish out to you. But no one creates our moods except ourselves and no one deserves any consequences. We alone are responsible for our feelings and our behaviour. It is quite a problem this habit of accusing others of creating our feelings and behaviour, because it backfires when they then retaliate silently or loudly, overtly or covertly, and we set up an unwanted chain of reactions that we assume ourselves to be the victim of. Our moods are a product of our feelings. Our feelings are a product of our expectations. Our expectations are a product of the 'reality' we have chosen as true. Our behaviour is our choice. It's the way we've decided to handle the situation.

No one else has control over the way we feel and behave unless we give them that control, unless we allow ourselves to be a helpless victim of their moods, behaviour and words. While we continue to think that other people control our feelings and behaviours, we are giving away control over our circumstances, and that leaves us very vulnerable to all sorts of negative things. It is no wonder that so many people begin to suffer depression, despondency and learned helplessness. We can feel trapped or frustrated or overwhelmed, thinking that other people are making our lives a misery.

Once we assume control of ourselves, we tap into a whole new world of potential within us. We realise that what we once thought was limiting us, exists only in our minds. We can become and grow into anything that is humanly possible. If we want to, we can change into just about any kind of person, and be that for real. No more pretending. We can program any traits we like into our automatic response system. We can learn all kinds of new ways to behave, respond, think and be in the world. We can tolerate or confront anything and not get emotionally affected at all. We can examine any input and refuse to accept it, or we can accept it but refuse to respond. The choice is ours, and the choices are vast in number.

Another way of describing this programming is to call it baggage. Here is an excerpt from an essay to explain it in a different way for you.

Shed the baggage

The only way to fix a miserable, failing life is to give up hope, throw in the towel, jump off the ladder and land on the floor. Give up completely and start again. You've tried your very, very best doing it a certain way and it's not working, so it's time to stop doing it that way and try something completely different.

What happens in life is that we collect all kinds of baggage as we go along. Baggage we think we'll need later. This baggage is made up of things like opinions, lessons, perceptions, feelings and conclusions and they largely make up the person we are. Because of our insecurity, we cling to all our baggage and keep trying to use it to help us find the answers. Because we have gone through so much and worked so hard to collect it all, we call it 'experience' and we blame other people and our circumstances for our failures. We are so sure that our baggage equips us to make clear judgements and to see things objectively that we never question ourselves.

The baggage itself is what is weighing us down and making us miserable. It is causing us to see things the way we do. It is causing us to think, behave, respond and react the way we do. Other people then treat us the way they do in response to the way we are.

Think of a situation at home or at work that really upset you recently. Now imagine you were someone else you know who would have handled the situation very differently. Imagine how different the outcome would have been if you were someone else entirely. You see what I mean? The rest of the world is not at fault, we are at fault for trusting our baggage.

You can surrender. You can give up, shed your baggage and start all over again. You can sit back, look around you and question the way you 'see' things. You can look objectively at all your baggage, your years of experience, and see what doesn't work. But you won't have the courage to do that until you have the courage to admit to being wrong. The reason it is so difficult to do this is that if we admit we are wrong, we face some scary things. Human beings generally hate being wrong. We may lose face, or feel empty and confused. We may have to face having dished out some serious consequences to others because we thought at the time that they were wrong. We might have to face humility or embarrassment or regret.

Some things like quick temper, lethargy or being easily offended, are nothing more than results of bad baggage. It is only hard to shed them as long as you keep using them. They are not your nature, they are merely bad habits you picked up somewhere along the way, and you can change them and exchange them for good, carefully chosen habits that are far more worthy of you. You can pick ones that get you the kind of effective results you want in life.

Ultimate Freedom – a state of mind and being

Ultimate freedom is something that bubbles up from inside us when we finally manage to let go of fear, hurt, guilt, jealousy and resentment. Easier said than done, I hear you say. The best way to let go of all of those negative feelings in one fell swoop is to let go of rationalizations, justifications, explanations and judgements - because these are all closer to our free will, and far easier to consciously choose to let go of. Plus, these are the root cause of those in the first list.

See nothing as 'better' or 'worse' than anything else. See no one as 'good' or 'bad', and know that every human being is always doing what he or she thinks is the best choice, or the only choice, available to them. Be like an excited child experiencing everything for the first time with no understanding of right or wrong. Want things to be as they are, and want what you have. Enjoy that which is already yours.

With trust and innocence, allow yourself to free fall. Have no ego. Never justify or defend yourself. Allow all and any opinions on earth. Be fascinated not irritated. Never try to be important. Never try hard to please. Never try to be more or less than what you are. Just slowly and steadily improve something each day and keep growing, for whatever is not growing is dying.

You are a child of the universe and you have a right to be here and you owe nobody anything. Relax and just exist in peace in whatever space you feel like. For as you try to be what you think others expect you to be, you make yourself uncomfortable or nervous which makes them uncomfortable or nervous with you.

Find your happy space and stay in it. If you do this, you will radiate positive energy and that will put others into a happy space too. Life is really great when everyone around you is in a positive happy space. You have already felt every negative feeling, and thought every negative thought. There is no reason to re-experience these again. You've been there, done that and got the T-shirt.

You have pondered, rationalized and reasoned all the sad, bad and painful things on earth and discovered that such pondering, rationalizing and reasoning failed to make even the slightest improvement on any of it. All it did was make you feel worse and multiply the original negativity and hurt. Every time you run the mental movie, you feel all those bad feelings again. What on earth for?

Step out of darkness and despair and step into light, joy and humour. Just do it. 'Justice' is darkness's greatest trick and trap. Believing that an injustice has been done causes us to think, feel and nurture darkness. In the name of good things like honesty, integrity and love, we soak ourselves in hatred and condemnation, hating and condemning those who hated and condemned! Isn't this ridiculous?

As we think about or discuss all these dark things we are accusing others' of doing, the darkness and negativity is in fact right then living and growing in us. In that very process we are creating it and spreading it. The suffering and dis-ease is happening in us, not the accused perpetrator. We make ourselves dark and miserable by contemplating evil, and all in the name of justice.

Do not chase after the poisonous snake that bites you and do not take up arms against the soldier or rush out with your stick against the lion to avenge the buck. Attempting to fight evil with evil only causes us to cultivate evil within ourselves. This will make us sick, angry, depressed and filled with despair and indignation - which will do us far more damage than the original offence. And it lasts so very much longer.

People are only actors on your stage. All you have of them is the pictures your eyes take and the recordings your ears take. Your brain may assign whatever meanings it likes according to your choice. You live with your choice whatever that may be. Your experience of life is created by the meanings you choose to assign to the people and events you encounter. Your feelings, thoughts and actions come from your meanings.

When we see people in a bad light, for whatever reason, we will be sending them signals of dislike or intolerance. We can sense each others' signals of dislike or intolerance, and we respond accordingly. So others will respond negatively to you in response to your negative signals. This is how we create our own environment and others' responses to us. We teach people how to treat us.

Choose to offer acceptance, non-judgement, love, light and humour to everyone - deserving or not - and you will give yourself the biggest gift life can possible offer. Love the world and it loves you back. Create the kind of stage you want to live and play in. It is entirely within your ability and control. This world is your playground, your practice field, your stage, and you can create whatever life you so desire.

Never give up on the dream you're chasing.
Never give in to your fears.
Sooner or later the fog will blind you,
Sooner or later it clears.

You are the one who determines your value.
Choose what you want with your years.
Learn anything that you want to be knowing,
You are the hearer that hears.

You are the one who decides to be happy
Or be a victim of tears.
Nobody else can live your life for you,
You are your vehicle that steers.

by Terri Ann Laws

Controlling vs. Allowing

I'd like to add a little piece here for all the control freaks, and if you are one, then I hope you find this useful.

We all need leaders and managers that are able to control people in certain areas and for certain reasons. A high price is fetched for such people in the market place. This ability can be useful in many ways. Parents need to control their children. The riot squad need to control the strikers. But controlling can be destructive if you assume the right to boss others around, find fault with them or their methods, or try to get others to do or to be what you want them to be (see Allowing).

Obviously we want to control as much of our own lives as we possibly can, but we should never try to control anyone else's life. We hate it when others tell us what to do, how to do it, how or what to feel, what to say and what to think. We hate being accused, dictated to and expected from. Yet so often we do this to others without realising that it can be insulting, offensive or just plain bossy. We want others to do the 'right' thing or do it the 'right' way, but actually that is insinuating that they are stupid and inferior to us - i.e. we know better than they do. This leads to a lot of bad feelings. It can damage people's self esteem and wreak havoc on relationships. Believing in the good and the capability and competence of others, even though they do things differently, is an act of trust that reaps great rewards.

The more we boss others around, are judgemental and find fault with others (in thought or in deed), the more we tend to justify and defend ourselves, and we become self-righteous. When we are able to allow others to be themselves we find we are more able to let ourselves be

33

ourselves too. The less we look to correct others, the more we accept ourselves. The less we find fault in others, the less we feel compelled to defend, justify and cover up faults in ourselves. There is tremendous freedom in being laid back and accepting and in just letting go and allowing. Remember, even God allows things!

Control freaks can be the worst perpetrators of self-criticism and self-condemnation, and this form of self-abuse is detrimental to your growth as a person. The child the teacher is always picking on and punishing, never improves, and in fact gets worse. The child the teacher encourages and is proud of gets better and better. This is true of all humans of any age, and we have to allow others to be who they are and be good to ourselves in order to remain encouraged and at peace in the world.

Let me close this chapter then by saying, do not lose hope if a particular trait seems too deep to budge. Some are tougher than others. It could just be that you picked the hardest one first, so leave that one for later when you have gained more experience and momentum, and start on an easier one instead. Remember, you don't have to change a darn thing about yourself. This is entirely a matter of choice. It will enormously improve your life, but it remains forever your choice. There is always somebody who will love you, warts and all, no matter how many warts you might have. If you really feel bad about it but don't want to change, you can always look for a partner that has a lot more warts than you have.

Best wishes, and may the force of peace and joy be with you.

Every point of refuge, so comforting, so nice,
Might be so relieving, but always has a price.

Every thrilling moment, that makes you want to sing,
Lurking in its shadow, holds a nasty sting.

Life cannot be easy, unless it's also hard,
And every joyous lifetime, is battered, bruised and scarred.

The reason for this seeming, unjust trick of life,
Is no one can be grateful, without a little strife.

'Tis only when the bitter, bad and hurting goes
We realise just how lovely, is goodness when it flows.

Only when we conquer our worries, hates and fears,
Can we guarantee ourselves, truly happy years.

by Terri Ann Laws

35

The 'Child' Within

Games

People play games. People put on an act. We all know this. Yet we also know that there are some authentic individuals out there who are straight down the line and clearly what you see is what you get.

When people behave in a certain way to achieve a certain effect, or when they change their behaviour, tone of voice and manner for a reason, they are actually acting, or playing 'games'. When we were small, this acting was done on purpose, but over the years the behaviour becomes automatic and we are no longer aware of doing it. A whole study has been done on this phenomenon. I first came across this idea in the book, *Why am I afraid to tell you who I am?*, by John Powell, and then later in the seminal book, *Games People Play by* Eric Berne, the father of Transactional Analysis therapy, or TA as it is commonly referred to.

We all play games to a greater or a lesser degree, although most of us don't realise it. As I describe the different types of games we play, you'll see what I mean. The object of a game is always to gain something, to avoid something or to control something (or someone). They are seldom fun, and they are neither good nor bad. They are survival tactics.

I have made sense of this study in my own way, and it is a little different from the traditional way the subject is taught, but this seems to me to be the most practically useful for most people.

Personality games

Playing the wounded bird, the victim, the bully, the clown, the 'know it all', or the silent observer are examples of personality games. The point of these games is to either avoid or to gain a certain reaction or response from others in a given context or for a specific reason.

For example, if I have severely reprimanded my son and later I see him depressed and in tears, I change from the angry ogre into the comforting mum. My entire personality changes as I try to repair the damage I have evidently done when I was attempting to correct certain wrong behaviour. I am not the same person I was earlier when I was angry with him. Personality games are various changes in our personality that we swing to for different reasons or effects at different times, and are not really a fixed part of our character. A personality played out of character could be called a 'personality game'.

Character games

Some people adopt a semi-permanent stance of wounded bird, victim, bully or clown, and remain in this role a lot of the time. They send out messages to the world, constantly saying, 'Treat me gently,' 'Take care of me,' 'Feel sorry for me,' 'Find me funny,' and so on. Other character games are things like: 'Aren't I fun,' or 'I'm dangerous, don't come close!' Character games are more like deeply embedded habits than occasional lapses into a different persona.

Paradoxically, character games are usually an indication of the opposite inner conviction. A bully, for example, is usually only playing the bully because he is terrified of being a victim. His only form of defence is attack. He thinks if he puts on a mean exterior, no one will dare hurt him. The clown is often afraid of being ignored or overlooked or laughed at. So he deliberately tries to make people laugh on purpose.

Social games
In the name of politeness, we are taught to be really fake when we are small. We say 'How are you?', when we really don't want to know. We are taught to smile sweetly and say something polite, even if we are angry with the person or don't like them at all. These social games ease social interaction and keep us what society calls 'civilised'. The games go further than this though. We can have shallow, meaningless conversations with people we would rather not talk to, we can 'act' bigger or smaller, extrovert or more reserved; we pose, pretend and try to be socially acceptable and polite, even if we're being utterly insincere, all because we feel obliged to conform to the 'proper behaviour' or the appropriate political correctness of the situation.

We use social games as a temporary 'show' to get us by and to get us through the awkwardness of encounters or to help us cope when we are among strangers to win favour. For some reason we feel we would be better off or safer if we act a part or put on a front than just be real and be ourselves. Social games are the games we play for strangers, and they also protect us from self-exposure and self-disclosure.

Life games

Some people have arranged their lives, and everyone in it, to perpetuate a game that they have formed in order to feel as though they have some control over a very scary world. Life games are an extension of character games, and they involve willing others, whether those others are aware of their participation or not.

Alcoholics, for example, find a partner who is a rescuer, a buddy who is an instigator, a boss or spouse or relative or someone else to be the perpetrator, and lastly, a friendly barman to take all these troubles to. He then has all these excuses and traps in his life so that he is 'forced' to keep on drinking. Actually, he drinks to escape responsibility because he is afraid of failure, afraid of life or perhaps too lazy or demoralised to bother even trying to win at the game of success. However, with his alcoholic game intact, he does not have to face the real reason for his drinking, and the drink keeps him anaesthetized too. He has the players and their various roles to hide behind.

A battered wife finally manages to rid herself of and divorce the abusive husband, only to have in time, her new husband turn abusive on her too. A person leaves their job because of the way their boss treats them, only to find in time that the new boss begins treating them the same way. This is because the game is inside the player, not inside the world, although the player might consciously believe that the world is causing the problem.

To perpetuate our life game, we choose our friends and acquaintances from people we like, the people we feel we relate to. These are the people who respond to us in a way that matches our frame of reference, our game. These are the people that do, say and react in the ways we instinctively can tell will fit our game. At the same time, we find we don't really like or connect with people whose behaviour does not fit our game. A domineering person will surround himself with people who are willing to be dominated. A victim will surround himself with perpetrators to complain about, and other victims to complain with.

Partnership games

Most of us select our partners because we recognize something familiar about them, and that warm recognition causes close feelings of affection to develop. This is how we almost inevitably end up with a partner who will play the complementary game to the one we play. For example, a man who feels driven to be strong and successful may look for a girl who has little hope of achieving much success because he wants someone who will never compete with him, but will instead be incredibly proud of him and awe struck by his greatness.

His first few choices may not work out because he may be choosing girls who feel inferior to him, rather than awe inspired by him. As soon as he finds someone who plays the right game, in the right way, he falls in love and gets married.

Subconsciously we all have some idea of what we want or need and so our attention is drawn to people who seem to be a certain way or have certain qualities. Somewhere between our comfort zone, where we think we fit in, and what we hope to get out of life, lies the formula for choosing our partner. It is difficult to draw this information out of our subconscious mind and become consciously aware of it, but this is an essential step if we find we keep picking the 'wrong' partners in life.

When two people fall in love with each other, it's because they can play the game of love that they are both comfortable with, with each other - even if that comfort zone is one of vicious fighting. When one partner grows out of a game, the relationship is doomed unless the other also grows out of it. For the game to work, both have to play their respective roles predictably and remain in the partnership or game comfort zone. People, who are very unhappy, often wish desperately that their partner would change, unaware that the game is being played in their own heads. If they change themselves, everything else will change, and the partner will either change or leave, and the game will collapse.

Ego states

Transactional analysis has also defined 'ego states'. The original idea of ego, or id, being the unconscious driving self, wanting to satisfy its own ego needs, comes from Freud. Various psychologists over the years have used it in slightly differing ways, but essentially to mean the same thing. As the metaphor goes, we all have ego states, and TA has identified three: child, adult and parent. I have adapted the basic TA model somewhat to my way of thinking. So, the child and the parent each have two different sides as they do in TA, but I have labelled them differently. The adult has only one side. The adult is always just the adult - reasoning, rational and centred — with common sense and intelligence, almost void of emotion. The child and the parent carry most of the emotion

Imagine a conversation between two people. One person makes a statement or a request. An onlooker can decide if that statement or request is the kind a rational, mature adult would make, or is it more the kind of statement a teenager, child or parent would make? The person spoken to then replies. Again, an onlooker could evaluate the response and decide if it is the kind of response one might normally expect from a rational, mature adult, or is it more like the kind of response one might expect from a teenager, a child or a parent.

You can listen to people interacting at the office or at home, and it is really interesting to listen with TA ears. It is so revealing of the relationships people have with each other unconsciously. A domineering boss often elicits childish, reactive responses from the full-grown adults who answer to him/her. A man can speak like a small child to his wife without even realising he is doing it when he says to her pitifully, 'My blue trousers aren't in my cupboard. I need them. Where are my blue trousers?' If she wasn't there, he'd look for his blue trousers himself, but 'mummy', i.e. his wife, is there, so he bleats to her for help.

The child
The natural child is that side of us that is playful, adventurous, cute, inquisitive and fun. This natural child is very often the best part of our personality. When we are in the natural child state, we feel free, happy and joyful. It is

good advice to tell those who suffer from stress and panic to indulge and nurture the natural child within themselves, because the natural child has the ability to see deadly serious challenges as exciting and adventurous or funny. The natural child is rich in positive emotion. May you discover your natural child and have lots of fun with it.

The taught child is that side of us that can be rebellious, obnoxious, anxious, afraid, resentful, sulky, retaliatory, a bit of tattle tail and full of complexes. The taught child is often the part of us that carries most of the damage we have suffered as children. The taught child also carries our induced conscience (early social brainwashing) and our fixed ideas about right and wrong; about justice and what is fair. The taught child is often the side of us that gives us the most trouble. If ever you see people behaving childishly or reactively, it is usually because the taught child has taken the stage and is making the decisions. Becoming depressed or manic is again the taught child running amuck.

We could use the 'adult' in us to get us out of that state, but the adult is seldom able to get control over the taught child or its state. It requires the natural parent in us to do that. No amount of intellectual reasoning is likely to heal a person of such afflictions, as most of us have realised only too well. In fact 'knowing' we should not feel or act this way or that way, often makes the problem worse because of the negative self-judgements that lead us into suffering self-condemnation and guilt. What we need our adult capacity for is to realise that we need to strengthen the natural parent and the natural child within us in order to disempower our taught child and taught parent. The taught child is swamped with negative emotion.

The adult

The adult is our mature, reasoning, rational, level-headed side. When we behave in a fully mature manner as a functioning adult, we make the best decisions for the best long-term outcome for ourselves and in general. People who are successful, balanced and completely mentally healthy have a strong adult ego state, and the capacity to choose this ego state at will. This does not come as a consequence of strengthening the adult state only. It comes consequentially from learning, healing and nurturing the 'damaged' parts of us as well, while growing our character and our consciousness, and of course also applying a lot of common sense.

Only a small percentage of the population manage to maintain and use at will a strong healthy adult ego state. Most of us have far too strong a taught child or taught parent in us which seems to take over far more often than we'd like. Whenever we are emotionally charged for any reason, most people find it difficult to remain completely adult and level- headed about things, without reacting.

The parent

There are also two parents, the natural parent and the taught parent. The taught parent comes from mental tape recordings of our own parents and other adults who raised and trained us and takes on all of their behaviour - functional as well as dysfunctional.

When in taught-parent mode, we are thinking and behaving as our parents (and others in authority from our youth) did. This side contains our controlling, dominating, prejudiced and stubborn behaviour. It also, like the taught child, holds all the rules and 'rights' and 'wrongs'. It can be complacent, worrying, complaining, judgemental, controlling, despairing, bossy and critical or any other behaviour we witnessed in our caretakers when we were young. The taught parent has a lot of different negative emotions.

The natural parent is our nurturing and caretaking side. It contains our instinctive capacity to protect, help and take responsibility for the welfare and safety of others and to be a good leader. It also contains a lot of our wisdom, gut feel, intuition, guidance and our feelings of universal love. The natural parent has all the positive qualities of a well-functioning parent and can use these with anyone in any situation. We need the natural parent to heal the taught child. Strengthening the natural parent in us will also improve our ability to be good leaders. The natural parent has strong, protective, positive emotions.

Once we can identify our behaviour and track where it is coming from, we can make huge improvements to our lives and the lives of others around us. It's wonderful to realise that we can gain so much more control quickly over many of our circumstances by understanding that reacting with a different ego state can significantly change the results we've been getting. All of our dysfunctional behaviour is simply various learned responses over time, and can be changed by understanding 'who' in us is taking over, and why.

In time, we want to dispense with most of the taught child and most of the taught parent. We want to increase our natural child, natural parent and adult sides to fill the gaps. To decide which ego state to work on improving or disempowering, we need to go through quite a lot of self-discovery, as I've said before. The input and honest feedback of others can be a great help, if we can be courageous enough to allow it. The direction we choose in life, our choice of vocation, will want some part of us to be specifically developed in order for us to excel in that particular field. For example, the caring profession wants a strong natural parent, while business requires a strong adult and the arts require a strong natural child.

You can change the dynamics of any relationship quite dramatically just by responding from a different ego state. People can become quite confused when they are used to you responding with a particular ego state and then suddenly you respond from a totally different place, with totally different types of words in a totally different tone of voice. Try it sometime. It can be most amusing.

The child within
You might want to know how to discover the natural child within, since a lot of people have long since lost touch with it. There is a simple process you can do. It is called Timeline Tracking. It has lots of other names too, copyrighted by various individuals for business purposes over the years, but whatever name you give it, it amounts to the same thing. This is what you do:

Think to yourself, if you were going to map your life out on some kind of line like a ruler or tape measure or road or railway track or something similar, so it started at your birth and ran in linear time up to now and then on to the future, what kind of line would seem right for you to do that on? Some people choose a neon light strip in some bright colour, others have a river or cosmic jet stream through space or some just a plain old line. Close your eyes and see what representation looks or feels right for you.

When you've done that, travel back along it in your mind and look for all the significant emotional events, the great highlights as well as the horrible shocks, that have shaped you over the years, and put some kind of a marker on each one. One client told me she'd imagined a railway track and all the big events were stations. Some were great buildings where a multitude of other railway lines crossed, and others were little tiny wayside stops with a small building in the middle of nowhere. Some were places she'd love to go to again, and others were places she never wanted to go back to. I liked that metaphor.

So, when you've made a timeline for tracking your past self, travel back along it in your mind to find the things you loved to do most when you were very small. Create memories around that, and pretend you are that age again, then imagine yourself having some really fun-loving, amazing adults taking care of you for the day and allowing you to have, be and do whatever you like, and then immerse yourself in the experience. You can indulge yourself and really enjoy being two or three or eight or whatever age you wish, doing all the things you love to do most. Imagine yourself laughing, running, screaming and charging around. Imagine yourself drawing or showing off or playing sport or anything you like, anything you loved to do back then, and add all kinds of details, even details that weren't there. This will re-awaken the natural child.

Practise doing this and soon you'll get very good at it, and you'll open your eyes each morning feeling wonderful, playful, spontaneous and full of youthful vigour.

Attracting

The art of attracting says that we attract to ourselves what we think about all the time. Every successful person has become that way because they think about success all the time. They get emotionally excited about all the wonderful things they are going to achieve before they've even achieved them. Everyone who has ever failed has done so because they thought about failure. Usually they put a lot of emotionally charged thought into the fear of failing and imagined in graphic detail how awful that would be.

If you keep thinking negative thoughts, you may well spend your life avoiding what you don't want, instead of attracting what you do want. The world sets out to prove to us exactly what we think is true. Our thinking sets up all our circumstances. Fun, happy people find the world a fun, happy place. Critical morbid people find the world a critical morbid place. Tight-fisted people find everything too expensive. Victims never run out of perpetrators. Our thinking is attracting more of the same to us all the time. As the saying goes:

Watch your thoughts, they become your words.
Watch your words, they become your actions.
Watch your actions, they become your habits.
Watch your habits, they create your destiny.

You can get a good look at your thinking by examining your circumstances. To begin with, try asking yourself the following questions, and see what you come up with?

- What do you spend most of your day thinking about? What keeps on showing up in your life?
- What have you attracted into your life?
- Do you realise how you attracted it?
- What have you attracted on purpose, and what was unwittingly?
- What thinking of yours will have to be permanently removed before your life can change?
- What thoughts will you have to add or increase before your life can change?

You already know that when you are in a good mood, you think about very different things than you do when you are in bad mood. And you also know that good luck is far more abundant when you are in a good space, and bad luck is far more abundant when you are in a bad space. Think about it: the person you are creates what you think about and what you think about creates the person you are. As you change your thoughts, other things about you begin to change; your posture, your tone of voice, the look on your face, your whole attitude, your actions, your choices, the way other people respond to you, everything.

If you are like most people, you enjoy the company of people in a good space more than the company of people in a bad space. Anyone will give a job sooner to a person with positive words and attitude than they will to someone with negative ones, even if the negative one is more qualified. Our thoughts are the only place we get our words from, and our thoughts are the only place we get our attitudes and our actions from. We think first and decide from there.

So the question to ask yourself is, what thoughts do you need to consistently think all day that will eventually get you where you want to be? Conversely, what thoughts are likely to do the very opposite? The art of attraction is working for you whether you want it to or not. People are meeting you, seeing you, talking to you, every day in person, on the phone, by email, and each and every interaction you make will have some kind of ripple effect in your life, big or small. Every thought you have has some effect. So, it makes sense to ensure that you are always thinking (and therefore attracting) what you *do* want, and not thinking (and therefore attracting) what you *don't* want.

I battled through the rivers wide
And thrashed upon the swelling tide
Expecting danger every turn
Finding misery to learn

Blaming debris, rocks and wet
Cursing, kicking, crying yet
Doing naught but struggling on
Suffering the journey long

Until I saw a happy seal
Frolicking with joyful zeal
Playing with debris, dodging rocks
Choosing when to dive or dock

Then I saw the journey fine
And learned to swim and dive in time
Then with debris built a boat
Now over all the rocks I float.

By Terri Ann Laws

51

You might have noticed how those people who are miserable and dismal seem to attract one unfortunate disaster after another. Have you ever wondered why some people get so much bad luck and suffer so many unfortunate things? It is an interesting question, and the law of attraction tells us it is because their consistent thoughts that precede all their choices, words and attitudes are attracting the very things they keep thinking about, and passionately thinking about with emotion. It is also mostly what they talk about.

You might also have noticed how the happy, joyful, positive people seem to get an unfairly large share of all the good luck and good things! Maybe 'fairness' has nothing to do with it, but thinking has everything to do with it. If I was emigrating and had a car to give away, I'd much sooner give it to a happy, grateful, nice person than to a miserable, moaning, 'not nice' person, even if the latter was poorer and needed it more. Wouldn't you? It simply feels so much better to give things to positive, happy, grateful people and it doesn't feel good to give to people who have a long face and a bad attitude, who moan and whine and assume the world owes them a living. It's a fact, and it is the reason why the positive happy people get so much good luck all the time, even when they don't really need it.

A small amount of random luck and disaster falls on the unsuspecting occasionally anyway, but fun, happy, positive people seem to attract huge amounts of the good luck and opportunities, and very few disasters and bad luck in their lives. When they do encounter bad luck or disasters they try to make the most of the situation. Many people rise up to help them, and they recover quickly. Often they even recount these tales in a humorous way, or as an entertaining epic story, and that is quite different from the morbid, victimized way the moaners and miserable people do it.

The law of attraction is also happening to those around us, including those we live close to, and sometimes their bad attracting can bounce off on us. This is not good. Since we can be in the line of fire, or in the same building, it can make us vulnerable. So, it is probably a good idea to encourage those people closest to you think happy and positive thoughts too and refuse to engage in conversation whenever the topic drifts on to ugly matters and issues.

When bad vibes or bad things are happening around us, we should say, 'Hey! I'm not attracting that! That's not on my shopping list! I'm going to ignore that. Someone else here must have ordered it.' Then carry on being your happy, cheery self. Once we have an awareness of this we can be sure to not absorb what we don't want. Another choice is to do what those from 'A Course in Miracles' do, they say, 'I can choose peace instead of this.' Isn't that great?

Once you have a clear idea of what you do want, you can think about it, plan it, dream about it, talk about it, focus on it, imagine it all the time, and go out in search of ways to get it , get excited about it, attract more and more ideas, people, ways, methods and plans. That really kick-starts the law of attraction into working for you. In your imagination pretend you have it now, and enjoy daydreams. For example, if you imagined you had that beautiful new house, then whenever you have a bit of daydream time, you go into it in your mind, and paint one of the rooms, or replace a sofa or plant tulips in the garden.

That is how you use the art of attraction to get you whatever you want, and you really can have whatever you want. And it's important to not shoot yourself in the foot by thinking the opposite outcome half the time, or by entertaining doubts and imagining it won't or can't work.

We create our destiny according to our thinking
Note in the following practical day-to-day examples how thinking immediately effects the next moment:

- If we think we are 'worth less', we will speak and act as if we are 'worth less'. This will prompt others to see us as 'less than'. This will adversely affect our growth and opportunities.
- If we keep mulling over thoughts of wrongs or injustices done to us, we will be training ourselves to be resentful, negative people. We will soon speak, act and attract accordingly. Because we are already negative, angry or resentful, the slightest thing will set us off again.
- If we think our loved ones should be paying us more attention, we become sulky and demanding. While we keep thinking 'what about me?', they become demanding and start thinking 'What about me?'.
- If we think the task at hand is easy, we plough into it confidently. If we think it will be hard we hesitate, and if we lack confidence in our ability, we fumble and make mistakes, proving our fears to be right.
- If we think we can do it, we keep on trying, if we think we can't, we won't bother.

- When we think we deserve, we insist and make sure we get.
- If we think we are better than everyone else, we will always look down on everyone else. Imagine what effect that has!
- If we think we're out classed we'll feel inferior.
- If we think we're a winner, we'll always be proving it.

We can make things true in our lives just by our 'thinking'. We can choose what we want to believe is true. The true scientific facts in the world are only commonly held beliefs and facts change over time. Scientists take different things as true these days than they did a hundred years ago, or two hundred years ago. Even the encyclopaedia is updated every year.

We can question our facts and beliefs to see if it they are working for us. If we keep doing things the way we've always done them, then everything around us will remain the way it's always been. Our 'facts' are telling us what we need to do. If the 'facts', are resulting in us being miserable, nervous or suspicious, it would make sense to change our mindset by looking for contrary evidence to disprove our 'facts' so we can choose new ones. If other people who are happier than you believe differently, then obviously it is possible to believe differently and get different results as a consequence. If all people who believed differently to you were very much worse off and less happy, then you'd have a case for continuing to believe the 'truths' about things and the 'facts' about things that you hold.

If you keep thinking (attracting) negative thoughts, you may well spend your life trying to avoid Murphy's Law and self-fulfilling prophecies. You'll be too busy putting out fires to move on. Obviously you think your negative thoughts are true and valid, or you wouldn't have them. That's why, and that's how, they attract more of the same to you. Your faith and belief in them is what makes them work. The only reason your beliefs are true is because you believe them. Other people believe different things, and so they get different results in their life. We always look for evidence to prove what we already believe because we want to be right. This is human nature. Everyone thinks they are right no matter how enormously we all differ in what we believe is right. Sometimes when we win, we really lose, and sometimes choosing to be right means sacrificing happiness. This is an interesting and important thing to contemplate.

If I think something's funny what happens? I laugh. If I laugh what happens? Others around me laugh or cheer up. Being aware of this, I can attract happiness around me if I want it. I can choose to see the sunny side of everything. As Abraham Lincoln said, "People are about as happy as they make up their minds to be." I can smile and wave as I drive down the road and nine out of ten drivers will smile back. I can create a happy world to live in just by being happy all the time myself. Very soon all the miserable people will drift away, the cynics will abandon me, the negative moaners will not like me so much anymore and they'll go hang out somewhere else and the happy people will gravitate towards me. Before you know it, I'll be surrounded by happy people and I'll be living a happy life in a happy world.

If I think I've been insulted or slighted what happens? I feel bad, and I show it. I might sulk, withdraw, grumble, complain, get angry or whatever. If I do this, what happens? Others around me respond to it, they can't help it. So because of my reaction they might feel scared or tense or uneasy or they might argue or fight with me. Once I'm in this frame of mind and I've put everyone else into a bad frame of mind too, I'm surrounded by negativity and bad vibes and all sorts of things go wrong one after another. Sure, I could blame whoever or whatever upset me in the first place, but that won't change the situation. You can set yourself up to have a bad day by dwelling on the first bad thing that happens in the morning. Once aware of this, we can see how we are able to attract bad things and so can also be aware of the fact that we can change the situation just as quickly and just as easily.

The state we are in affects the state of everyone around us. You might have noticed how strongly people affect each other, even without speaking. Have you ever been around a person who is so calm and together and loving and happy that they exude gentle positive energy? It is as if anyone near them can feel totally relaxed because they hold a steady space of calm and comfort. If I can manage to remain totally relaxed, calm and feeling at home wherever I am, people around me will soon begin feel the same. As long as I stay in that state, I will be attracting that same peace around me wherever I go.

If I find the world a safe, relaxed, calm place, I will feel at home wherever I am. Others will feel comfortable and at home around me and, in fact because of me.

People tend to get what they set their minds to get, and they tend to not get the things they fear they'll not get, or feel bad about not getting, no matter how badly they want those things. Fear, worry and feeling of lack or expecting bad luck seems to push things away. A positive conviction and abundance mentality attracts good things towards. It may

57

not seem logical, but it definitely happens. Those who fail most often are those desperately trying not to fail. Those who win most often are those who expect to win and play to win.

Perhaps there has been a time in your life when you really, really wanted something and set forth with utter determination and didn't give up till you got it? When we want something badly enough and decide we're definitely going to have it, we begin thinking constantly of ways to get it. We imagine and plot and plan, we hope and wish and scheme, we keep doing different things, leaving no stone unturned. Our thoughts become focused very strongly.

The more we focus our thoughts, the more creative we become in dreaming up ideas and ways we might be able to get the thing we want. Our enthusiasm and commitment grows, and then coincidences and serendipity start occurring along with radically increased luck. There is no logical explanation of why this happens, but it always does. When you've made up your mind to get something, you get it.

This happens both positively and negatively depending on the direction of our focused thoughts. If you place intense emotion and deep, strong thought on bad things that happened or on revenge, jealousy, greed, spite, blame, whatever, the same force of attraction comes into play and you may notice you get bad coincidences and major bad luck. You are also likely to meet people who feel as you do and behave as you do. While you may feel they are a comfort to you, in fact they are strengthening the 'bad' for you much like you are strengthening the 'bad' for them. Birds of a feather flock together and attract for each other more of the same stuff they think about and talk about together.

Have a look at what you are attracting by looking at the scenarios you play and replay in your thoughts all day. What do you spend most the day thinking about?

- The things you want so badly?
- The fights you had?
- Wrongs done or said to you?
- The fun you've had?
- The places and people you enjoy?
- The falling economy or rising crime rate?
- Your children's bad points?
- Other people's bad points?
- Your limitations and things you can't do, things you wish you could do?
- Things you don't have?
- Lack, shortage, not enough?
- Painful past memories?
- The people you love?
- Running delightful memories of good times past and creating fantasies about all the fun things you could do?
- Huge, wonderful plans for your future?
- Ways to make money?
- All the terrible ways it is possible to lose money?
- Solutions to problems?

The list is endless. These are just a few of the millions of things a person could spend thought energy on. Each thought has magnetic power. Large amounts of similar thoughts have a much stronger magnetic power.

Do a mental check and track what you spend all your thought energy on. See what you are attracting. See how you are training yourself. All these thoughts are attracting what you are experiencing in life. All these thoughts are training you. They are forming habits and patterns. They are convincing you of all sorts of things. They are making you see yourself, others and the world at large in a certain light. You can only do things that you can see yourself doing. What do you keep seeing yourself doing? Are these the things you want to keep on doing? These are really important questions that we should regularly ask ourselves in order to remain consciously aware of the life we are creating for ourselves.

Simple steps to help you attract to yourself what you really want

Start thinking about something you want to bring into your life all the time. Start looking at it and imagine it as if you had it now. Imagine you already have it and enjoy the fantasies in detail. See yourself there with it or in it. Learn all about it. Keep on trying ways to get it. Every time you fail, look for the reasons why you failed, make some distinctions, and then try something else. Remember there is no failure, only results, and all results are useful feedback. Look, learn, think, feel, want, notice and network.

Go out and find out how to get what you want. Research, read, ask people, try things and do things. Practise positive expectancy and know you'll have it, and it's only a matter of when and how. Visualize it. Bring it into your comfort zone. Use all your resourcefulness and initiative. Attract it into your life with the power of your expecting, the power of your mind. Talk about it as though you already have it.

Make sure you genuinely feel you deserve it, that you have a right to have it, it is OK to have it, you have permission to have it, it is yours for the taking, you will have it and it is only a matter of how quickly can you get it. Then watch for the luck, the coincidences, the chance meetings and the things that just pop into your life from nowhere to help you get it.

Try it! What have you got to lose?

Value

How valuable are you?

If you want to know what you are worth, just look at your pay cheque. You chose that job and that direction. Would you even bother to apply for a job advertised in the newspaper that offered ten times the pay? You'd probably assume they wanted ten times the person you are. Your pay has got nothing to do with your skills and abilities but everything to do with the value you place on yourself. I know plenty of people who are very clever, very knowledgeable and very hard working who work for a pittance for a slave-driving boss. I also know lots of people who do very little all day and earn a fortune by employing the above mentioned types to do all their work for them.

If you want to know how valuable you are just look at how others treat you. You chose those people to be in your life, and you taught them how to treat you by speaking and behaving as you do. Notice how your children treat you.

You brought up your children and have been influencing them from birth. Blaming your spouse or others is not only pointless and futile, it is silly and irresponsible. The way they treat you is the way you taught them to, whether you did it deliberately or totally inadvertently. How does your boss treat you? How do your staff treat you? How do family members treat you? How do strangers treat you?

Seeing myself as valuable after the upbringing I had was a major challenge for me. I had to really think a lot and alter a lot of programming before I could answer these following questions and feel good about my answers.

- What is your basic value?
- What are you worth in the scheme of things?
- What do you deserve? Do you deserve to be paid £2,000, £20,000, £200,000 per month?
- Do you deserve to be loved and adored by people?
- Do you deserve to be respected?
- Do you deserve to be feared?
- Do you deserve to be waited on hand and foot?
- Are you special?
- Do you deserve to be overworked/rushed off your feet/underpaid?
- Do you deserve to be shouted at, resented or hated?
- Do you deserve to be ignored or laughed at?
- Do you deserve to be used and taken advantage of?
- Are you lucky to be allowed to live, or are others lucky to have you around?
- Do you deserve loyalty and devotion?

The truth is, it is *we ourselves* who decide what we are worth. *We* create our own value. Other people then respond with 90% predictability. No one else but we ourselves can decide how valuable we are. It is no one else's responsibility to decide your value for you. Sure it helps if someone believes in you and sees you as hugely valuable, as long as you can accept and believe in their belief in you. If you put yourself down enough, they will stop valuing you in time. We still need an intrinsic sense of being valuable before we can even believe that someone else's belief in us is based on good judgement and fact.

What are some of the other clues and tell- tale signs that let you know how valuable you believe yourself to be?

Well, if you were totally sure you were valuable you wouldn't take offence at anyone's criticism. In order to be hurt by what they say, you need to be starving for their good opinion of you. If I am starving for your good opinion of me, I must value your opinion more than I value myself.

People are only actors on your stage. If you don't have an intrinsic sense of your own value, then you'll want everyone else to place you high up on their stage. But that's plain ego and not realistic. You can't possibly have the same place on everyone else's stage, just as they can't all have the same place on yours. Obviously some people will place you lower and others will place you higher on their stage and that's normal and OK.

The funny thing is, when we put a huge value on ourselves, others put a bigger value on us too without even realising they are doing it. We come across as bigger and confident. We are also far more likely to put a bigger value on others because we are no longer comparing, defending or competing. People seem to sense this and respond favourably. It is easy to like people who seem to value you.

And when you value yourself, you won't care too much whether they like you or not, and then they will want you to like them because they like the confidence and ease they see in you. Everyone likes it when valuable people give them attention, and people always try to get the attention of valuable people. People who are valuable are those who have made themselves valuable.

Ego versus value

There is a big difference between having a big ego and having an intrinsic sense of your value.

- Ego has you thinking you are better than everyone else. Value has you knowing it.
- Ego has you proving or trying to prove it to everyone else. Value has you trying to show others how valuable they are too.
- Ego has you blaming and accusing everyone else, because the great 'I am' could never be at fault. Value has you taking responsibility and even blame and helping others to feel safe enough to take some too.
- Ego has you defending and justifying yourself at all costs. Value has you defending and justifying others and helping them feel OK.
- Ego has you placing yourself on a pedestal, looking down on everyone. Value has you pulling everyone up to share your pedestal with you.
- Ego has you trying to force people to value you. Value has you leaving the choice up to them.

If you are driven by ego, and others try to climb onto your pedestal, you tramp on their fingers and push them down, because you see them as a threat - trying to take your space. If you are driven by value and others try to climb onto your pedestal, you take their hands to help them up and make space for them. You help them build a pedestal for themselves.

Think about this:

> If I was completely sure I was valuable I could not take offence. I would take your actions and words as a statement about you. You could say or do anything to me and I would not be hurt by it, I would merely decide what kind of person you are. You could ignore me or dislike me and it wouldn't upset me. *Your opinion of me would not be able to hurt me!* If I need you to put value on me, I must on some level doubt myself, while not doubting your opinion. If I did not doubt myself, I would think something is wrong with you or I might allow you your opinion and think nothing of it.

Let's say that I have decided that being 'strong' is a fault and being 'kind and soft' is a virtue. Now, if you see me as a strong person, I could think that means you don't value me. If I value myself, I could be intrigued that I am coming across as a strong person to you, when I thought I was coming across as kind and soft. I could think about that and work on it, if my intrinsic sense of value was intact. If it hurt me that you saw me as strong when I wanted you to see me as soft and kind, I would remain stuck. I would probably defend and justify myself and try to convince you that you were wrong about me. I would try to change your opinion rather than try to change the way I come across.

I need to know that I am valuable either way. I need to feel safe and accepted before I can say, "Tell me what it is about me that makes you see a strong person when I think I'm being kind and soft?" If I feel valuable, if I am open, confident and free, I can ask you to explain how I'm acting or speaking that is making you see me as strong. I can listen with intent to understand, and I can thank you for telling me. I can learn something about you, about myself, and about our relationship. If I don't value myself, I will not be able to let you tell me. It would be too threatening for me because the truth hurts and I'd want you to tell me little white lies and pretend things are as I wish they were.

It is up to each one of us to decide what value we want to have, and what value we want others to see in us. If it is not your own personal decision then others hold your confidence and your happiness in their hands. Why would anyone else decide to make another person valuable? That's crazy. It simply doesn't work that way. Each person has to decide for themselves, and then let the world know.

It seems that it is only when we are unsure of our basic value as a person that we need reassurance from outside ourselves. We need others to tell us we are valuable only when we doubt ourselves. We are supposed to be deciding how valuable we are. Others have no say in it. Giving them a say makes us vulnerable. There seems to be a very strong connection between suffering a lack of feeling valuable and suffering jealousy, poor work performance, bad attitude, inner conflict and feeling victimised. We are also far more likely to criticise others when we ourselves doubt our own value.

So, we need to ask ourselves some serious soul-searching questions such as:

- Whose opinion of me is important and why am I allowing it to be important?
- Who do I choose to give power over me?
- Perhaps even so much power that their disapproval of me could destroy my confidence, my happiness and my life?
- Who am I answering to?
- Why am I answering to them?
- What am I getting out of it?
- Is there any benefit to me at all if I place huge importance on other people's judgement and opinions of me?
- Am I attracting disapproval into my life to reaffirm a deep subconscious belief that I am worth less?
- Good grief! I would never do that on purpose!
- Then I must make sure not to do it by mistake either.

Believe it or not, there actually are some people out there who enjoy feeling bad and enjoy nurturing the many victimisations they have suffered. They spend their inner dialogue time in fantasy stories of being the most hurt, misunderstood, abused, disrespected poor little thing on the planet and fantasise about being rescued and they fantasize sever awful punishments onto the people who have failed to pander to them or to please them, and to people who have hurt them. It sounds a bit sick, but there really are people like that. They get mileage out of making sure others don't value them.

It is a good idea to become a lot more sure of your value and your right to be here no matter who you are, no matter what anyone says, and no matter what anyone thinks of you.

A large amount of domestic and relationship fighting is based on value. When one says, "How dare you speak to me like that!" What they mean is they want the other to see them as more valuable. We need not take our family members' manners or opinions personally, even if they intended them personally. Nothing and no one can force anyone to take anything personally. They can certainly try, but if you don't respond as they intend you to, there is absolutely nothing they can do about it.

Your partner arrives late, forgets to phone and doesn't apologize. What you might feel is 'I'm not important enough.' What you could feel instead is, 'He is so scatterbrained, and if his head wasn't screwed on he would forget that too.' Or 'I have chosen for myself an unfocused, unreliable person to love.' Or 'She appears to have very little sense of commitment.' Anything rather than to take it as a sign that he or she doesn't value you.

Saying, 'Put a higher value on me or else', doesn't work. We can't tell other people to do that. It's a spontaneous thing that comes from the heart. We can only tell them to act as if they do or to 'say' they value us, which may necessitate them being fake or telling us lies. It always amazes me how many people force others to 'show them respect' or to 'show them love'. Do you really want others to fake it? To merely say they value you? To pretend they respect you or love you?

We can't tell others how or what to feel. We could get them to put a higher value on us by first putting a higher value on ourselves, and then putting a higher value on them. If we demand respect we get resentment, compliance or fear. If we earn respect we get love as well.

We should refuse to be a doormat or a victim because that decreases our value. We can defend ourselves by confronting with courage and consideration, by looking for a fair solution that everyone is happy with, and that will increase our value and improve the relationship.

How can you feel valuable to yourself? Well, remember you are the only person who can live this life for you. You have to take care of yourself, feed yourself, protect yourself, get yourself a job and a home. You have to find yourself love, friends and a partner. You are irreplaceably valuable to yourself. You can dispense with friends and family, but you can never dispense with yourself. At the end of the day, all you have is you! If you can't value yourself, you can never be truly happy. If you feel you have little value, you won't expect anyone to value you, and this will create a self-fulfilling prophecy. Make yourself the most valuable thing in the world!

Some ways to increase your sense of how valuable you are

- Make a list of all the things you can do, and all the things you have accomplished, even the little things.
- Do at least one thing every day that you don't want to do but have to do, or have been putting off doing for a long time. Then feel excellently good about yourself for doing it.
- Make a list of your shortcomings into two columns – one column for the things you don't want to change, and the other for things you do want to change. Then tackle those things one by one with diligence and patience. Feel fantastic every time you overcome a shortcoming you used to have.

- Increase your courage by confronting your fears little by little until they no longer scare you.
- Stop justifying and defending yourself. Stop explaining yourself to people.
- Believe in yourself. If you can't do something, know that you can learn.
- Do more. Take more action.
- Stop worrying about things outside of your control.
- Increase your willingness to be wrong, vulnerable, rejected and humble.
- Place a higher value on those beneath you and a lower value on those above you. Eventually close the gap completely.
- Have a compelling plan for the future, but don't fear or worry or fret about whether you can or can't achieve it. Be the very best you can be for this one day only.
- Learn from the past. Never dwell on negative past events. Do not waste a single thought on things you cannot change. Rather learn something good from it.
- Never feel compelled to tell lies. Either tell the truth or refuse to comment. Only lie if you want to and choose to for a good reason and not because you're afraid to tell the truth.
- Detach from other people's opinion of you.
- Stop pointing fingers at others, or yourself. Quit finding fault.
- Be willing to say sorry directly and make amends. This makes friendships stronger and goes a long way to dismantling foolish, defensive pride. It also drastically increases your courage with drastically increases your good opinion of yourself.
- Forgive yourself even if others don't.

- Let go of resentment and hard feelings. They keep you stuck and attract negativity.
- Assume everybody likes you. Think and act accordingly regardless because assuming people don't like you certainly wouldn't encourage them to.
- Never sell yourself short in an attempt to please others.
- Never let anyone make a victim or a scapegoat out of you. Put your hands on your hips, look them straight in the face and say absolutely nothing till they cringe and go away.
- Keep adding to this list yourself. You are the best person to ask the question 'How can I increase my value?'

Until you can convince yourself that you are valuable, you'll never be able to convince anyone else you are. Well, not for long anyway.

You are obviously very valuable. You only have to realise your value, by refraining from doing the things that make you feel less (the opposites of the above list). Remember, people are only actors on your stage. You assign them a place in your life. You decide how valuable they are in your life in relation to yourself. You can change their position and their role anyhow and anytime you like. This is your life; your experience and you can make of it whatever you want.

Imagine you are in a hospital. You walk past the nursery where all the tiny little newborn babies are asleep. Look at them. So innocent, so unsuspecting, so vulnerable and so helpless. Look at the one closest to you. It's cute little face. If it were in your power to do, what would you order for that little baby in its lifetime? Would you say it must get loving parents, the best of everything, a wonderful nature, a strong character, lots of friends, talents, abilities, success and money? If yes, then why? What has that baby done to deserve such a huge blessing? What great achievements or contributions has it made that determine what it deserves?

Nothing!

So why would you wish it so well?

It is a little baby, and just because it exists, it deserves the best things in life.

That baby is you. Now go out and get for yourself all the things you said that baby deserved. You are big now and you have the power. If that baby had a raw deal up till now then hurry up and make it up to him/her. You've got a lot of catching up to do. It's never too late to have a happy childhood and it's never too late to become a very valuable person. Just because we exist, we deserve.

A person who feels valuable is very good to others. They are patient, understanding, forgiving and allow everyone else to be just who they are because they have nothing to prove or to lose. It's only those who doubt their own value who try to devalue, punish or discredit others.

Please be with me when I'm down,
my shoulders drooped, my face in frown.

Please be with me when I'm high,
racing, spinning, flying by.

Please be with me when I'm sad
and seeing the world as cruel and bad.

Please be with me in my glee,
laughing, playing, singing free.

Please be with me in between,
when I'm kind and when I'm mean.

Through each passing mood and phase,
I always love you in all ways.

I will do the same for you,
so always you can love me too.

by Terri Ann Laws

Values and Rules

The value we place on words, behaviours, attitudes and things

We often live at variance with our values. This can cause us great stress. For example, you may value fitness, but hardly ever exercise or go to the gym. Some value university degrees, but don't start studying to get one. Some value honesty with people, but keep telling white lies for 'good' reasons. Some value adventures, but never leave the house. You may value love but see it as something you expect to receive rather than something you expect yourself to give. You may value and long for wealth but hate the rich.

The more we live at variance with our values, the more we find fault with others, and the worse we feel about our lives and ourselves. Having values that we keep violating creates in us tension, frustration, low self-esteem, or a judgemental, critical attitude. It's easier for us to see faults in other people than it is to see faults in ourselves. So we notice when others violate our values but we don't necessarily notice when we violate our values ourselves.

We value different things to different degrees. We put a huge value on some things and a lesser value on others.

I once knew some people who could not possibly respect a person who does not love classical music because to them a love of the classics means culture, and to them culture is the most valuable thing. To those people, since having culture (a love of classical music) is of utmost importance, it forms the basis of whether they accept or reject anyone they meet, without giving any other qualities a chance to show themselves. They put such a high value on it that they let it dictate every aspect of their existence, including where they will go and who they will speak to. They can be so blinded by this that they don't even realize that 'culture' is much more than classical music, and is country, race and area specific. What we value most highly has the potential to create massive blind spots.

Some people value adventure to such a degree that they regularly risk their lives and their security. They will compromise anything and anyone if offered a really thrilling and exciting adventure. They take unpaid leave. They regularly persuade their spouse to give them time out to go away, or they have remained single. They spend most of their money on it and it comprises most of what they talk about. They will risk anything at the drop of a hat for an adventure. They only work for the money to pay for adventures. They live in anticipation of the next one. Their whole reason for living is for the adventures that life has to offer.

Some people value security to such a massive degree that they spend their whole life in a job they don't like and that underpays them. They will work hours of overtime without being paid for it, afraid that complaining might jeopardize their job security. Some stay in a bad, abusive relationship for the security of being married or staying in their comfort zone. They will sacrifice anything for the sake of security. They will do anything or go anywhere if it offers them security.

If you have a powerfully driving value, it is best to know it. Knowing what you value, knowing what you are placing massive importance on will help you figure out how you created the life you're living. We all have values and we have some strong ones and some less strong ones, and the stronger the value the stronger it drives our choices and decisions.

What do you value?

List all the things you value. Choose the top ten and then re-write the list carefully in order of importance for you - from most important at the top, to least important at the bottom to create a hierarchy. You may be interested to know that this hierarchy determines your personality and your character and it predicts what you will and won't do. If security is at the top of your list and adventure is at the bottom, you probably won't go parachuting. If control is at the top, you probably have big trouble allowing. If friendliness and equality is at the top, you probably make friends with everyone.

Once you have your list of values in a hierarchy, see where your actual behaviour contradicts your values. For example, you may value making a contribution but struggle to part with a penny, and feel resentful when asked to help.

See which of your values contradict each other. For example, you value a social life, and you value family devotion. You love to go out often, and feel you should stay home with the kids often. Therefore you always feel guilty when you go out and deprived when you stay in.

See which behaviours and traits you greatly admire and see as very valuable in others, but never thought to learn and acquire them in or for yourself. What effect does this create for you? How does this affect your experience of life?

Decide what you want to value most in future - in line with what you actually do, or are committed to start doing.

Define all the *rules* connected to each of your values. Our rules are the specific words and actions that need to happen to show us a value is being met or violated. For example, 'respect' to one person might mean good manners and politeness, but to someone else it might be credit and recognition. To someone else respect might mean being honest and fair. Most words that constitute values are 'spooks' in that they have no definite meaning. They mean a different thing to each and every person.

This is why it is important to list your rules regarding each value, so you know what you mean by that value. It will then also be easier to explain your values to others. If you just use the 'spook' word, people might wholeheartedly agree with you, but have a very different picture in their head and neither or you knows it. Then you may be surprised or upset when they violate a value they agreed to honour. In fact they might well be honouring their interpretation of what that value 'word' means. All values need to be clearly defined in terms of the actual actions that mean that value.

Some examples might be:

- I value reading. The rules are: read one good book per week.
- I value generous people. The rules are: they give small change to beggars, give all old clothes away free of charge.
- I value helping others. The rules are: lend a maximum of £x. If they don't pay back, never lend

to that person again. Do a max of one favour per month per friend. Be available only for close friends and family.

You might have dozens of rules for some values. The values I've mentioned above may be vastly different from the kind of values you have in mind. The kind of rules that you imagine to be right or fair may be vastly different too. That's fine. The point is to find your values and your rules that determine your values, and then follow your own rules. It is far more important to follow your rules yourself than it is to get others to follow your rules. If you don't follow your own rules, you'll find it very difficult to get others to buy into them and cooperate with you. Ask any parent! Besides, getting others to follow your rules won't make you as happy as you thought it might, but following your own rules yourself certainly will.

Make the necessary changes and then live in harmony with your values. See where you find fault with others. When we judge others (or their actions/words), we do so from our beliefs and our values about what is right or wrong, and by what we think is important or necessary. They may have different beliefs. They may have very different values. They may have similar values but very different rules.

So often we judge ourselves by our intentions but we judge others by their actions or behaviour. This happens when (or because) we imagine everyone shares our values and beliefs, or should share them, since we feel certain that ours are the 'right' ones, the obvious facts and truth. If others don't share our values, then we feel sure they are ill informed or wrong or strange.

We sometimes place a higher value on our beliefs and values than we do on our relationships. Higher than the welfare of other people. This is how we create conflict. This is how we create wars. This is how we create divorce. We defend our beliefs, our values and our rules vehemently, and others defend theirs too. That's how all fighting happens. We forget how important the other person is and focus only on how important it is for us to be right and to show the other person to be wrong. But the other person is just as determined as you, and you both seriously damage the relationship in your extreme effort to be right. Once you've damaged the relationship, future clashes become much worse and even less cooperation and tolerance is available from both sides.

Allow others their values and rules and work only on yours with yourself and your life will improve dramatically.

On borrowed wings of liberty
I came to rest on purgatory,
And viewed the width of world
from way on high.

I keep helping many other,
While my own despair I smother,
As I bravely just work harder
'n will not cry.

An angel came with teachings
And he frowned upon my preachings,
And he said 'you should just
listen not reply.'

A rescuer came with money
And he said 'I'll help you honey,
If we can be special friends
just You and I.'

My leaking soul was emptying
And I found the offer tempting,
But I couldn't come to grips with
pride and why.

At last the layers are thinning,
And I think I'll soon be winning,
As I learn to think more clearly
by and by.

by Terri Ann Laws

Allowing

The art of allowing basically says:

"Stop bossing. Let go, chill out, live and let live."

Allow people to be whatever they are. If they are wrong or right, good or bad, informed or ignorant, on track or off track, what does it matter? Feeling compelled to correct people, disapprove of people or in any way interfere with people gets us involved in the act of controlling and/or judging. If you are in fact God or Allah, or if you are the supreme emperor of the world, then ignore this chapter, but if you are a human being living in a world with other human beings, then read on.

A lot of people tell me they can't allow others to be rude, obnoxious or offensive, so to them I ask, "Why not?" If others feel the need to let off steam, say nasty things, rant and rave like a baby, sulk, reject you, walk out, whatever, just let them. It is not good for you, nor does it make you happy, to jump in and join other people in their misery. Don't react to someone else's words, behaviour, choices or temper. That is their stuff. Don't take it on board. Most abuse happens after the victim has responded unwisely or ineffectively or inappropriately to the perpetrator's initial anger or antagonism. If they walked away immediately without responding or reacting at all, or just stood there looking at the person with a blank expression without saying a single word, then it can't escalate to the point where it gets nasty.

We are not our behaviour and other people are not their behaviour. Behaviour is only our learned response over time. Behaviour is a symptom. We can change our behaviour, but we cannot easily change anybody else's. We don't give anyone the right to tell us how to think, feel and act, so why do we think we have the right to tell others how to think, feel or act? What gives us the right to label people 'good' or 'bad', 'right' or 'wrong' according to the way they choose to think, feel or act?

Separate the person from their behaviour - then you can disapprove of the behaviour without disapproving of the person. Separate yourself from the whole scene and say to yourself, 'This person is obviously feeling some intense emotions right now.' Or 'What strange behaviour!' or 'What an unusual person!' Protect yourself by detaching and allowing the person to get on with their choices, performance or behaviour. Bad behaviour doesn't usually last long, unless we react to it.

When people do whatever it is they do, we imagine that they are doing those things to us. For example, 'He makes me jealous.' Or 'She makes me angry.' Or 'They do that to annoy me.' This is not accurate. They are merely doing those things. Their intentions are their problem, not yours. We choose our response. Sure they may be hoping their behaviour will cause us to become jealous or angry or annoyed, but the final choice of response is ours. They are not doing anything to us; they are merely doing things.

Allowing is the opposite of controlling. When we try to control people we cause jealousy, lies, insecurity, anger, bitterness, resentment, comparisons, disappointment, fighting, frustration, heartache, rejection and who knows what else. So why on earth do we do it? Every human being has a God-given right to be as evil or as good as they choose to be. We all have a free will. That's a sad fact, but a very true one. It is hard not to react when someone else behaves badly or strangely, but reacting seldom improves the situation. It just results in us including ourselves and usually makes things worse.

There is such tremendous freedom in just detaching and allowing. We completely remove other people's power to hurt or frustrate us. We will be really free and really happy when we learn to 'allow' ourselves. We will never be able to allow ourselves until we can allow others. Think of all the things you'd love to do, but wouldn't dare for fear of how others may react. They might laugh or get angry or think badly of us. We allow them to control us because we are not allowing ourselves to be whoever we are. Actually, we are controlling ourselves because of a fear of other people's reactions to us or thoughts about us.

Some of the ways we disallow ourselves

- We don't allow ourselves to feel certain feelings. (I shouldn't feel that way.)
- We fear to allow ourselves freedom of speech. (I shouldn't say that here/now.)
- We don't allow ourselves freedom to act. (I shouldn't do that here/now.)
- We feel bad, guilty, stupid or wrong after doing or saying something.
- We don't allow ourselves to try for fear of failing. (Don't want to look stupid.)
- We accuse ourselves of not being good at stuff - but we haven't allowed ourselves time to learn.

When we do any of these things we think we should not do, or are not allowed to do, we feel guilty, angry, embarrassed, depressed or just plain terrible - and this knocks our confidence and self-esteem.

Be fascinated, not irritated!

How could you have a single enemy in the world if you allow all people to be as foolish or as wise, as cruel or as kind, as agreeable or as disagreeable, as stupid or as clever, as funny or as boring as they want to be without making any judgement of them? Just take them as you find them and observe with compassion, empathy or fascination. Hold the space for them to be whoever and whatever they are, and be detached and fascinated as you observe. Once you can do this for others, you'll be able to do it for yourself, and believe me, life takes on a whole new meaning then.

Allowing says, while I am free to attract whatever I want into my life, so is everyone else free to attract into their lives whatever they want in theirs. I do not do them a favour if I interfere or play God in their lives. I do not do myself a favour if I jump into their ring with them either. I help neither them nor myself if I interfere with what they are attracting. People don't want un-asked-for advice no matter how wise and good we might think it is.

There are other choices available to us. In fact we have many, many choices and the choice we make determines the next moment. For example: someone starts shouting and pointing at me. What should I do?

- I could take offence and get upset.
- I could politely tell them they are doing the wrong thing.
- I could stop them firmly and put them in their place.
- I could start shouting and pointing back.
- I could walk out and ignore them.
- I could try my best to placate them and help them calm down.
- I could start justifying myself and tell them it's not my fault.
- I could burst into tears and manipulate them into comforting me.
- I could run off and fetch my big body-builder friend to teach them a lesson.

I could do a large number of things, but all of the above are reactions to someone else's choices. They are all controlling instead of allowing.

In dealing with other people's rudeness or anger you need to remember that you are attracting into your life what you need, and if this behaviour is not on your shopping list, then don't take it and pay for it. If it is not yours, then it's none of your business and you'd be wise to realise that. There are other responses you might choose. There are healthier conclusions you can draw. For example, you could think...

This person is obviously having some trouble with their emotions right now. I am going to allow them, but I am not going to take it on board. My opinion of myself is perfectly intact, so their opinion of me is not going to alter that right now. It is pointless fighting or arguing with a person when they are in a bad state and not able to reason. Whatever I say now is only going to fuel the fire, if not without, then definitely within.

A friend of mine used to respond in a very interesting way. She used to put a pious, disapproving look on her face, put her hands on her hips and say, "Excuse me, is it appropriate for you to be this way?"

People are more likely to listen to what you have to say about it if you listen to them first, if you allow them to be who they are right then. You can easily tell them that you will listen to them uninterrupted until they are finished, and in exchange, you'll expect them to then listen to you uninterrupted, and neither one of you is expected to be convinced by the other, but both of you are prepared to fully listen to and hear each other.

*It's funny how the evil ghost
of anger lingers near,
keeping close to all his mates
like hurt and spite and fear.*

*Oh they try in many ways
to sow their ugly seeds,
wanting you to jump on board
so that you'll do their deeds!*

by Terri Ann Laws

I think the whole idea of *please* and *thank you* was supposed to stop humans from telling each other what to do. People still order each other around and try to get away with it by being polite with a *please* or *thank you*, so instead of ordering them to do it, we try to manipulate them into doing it. Remember that 'please' means - 'you have the choice to say no'. Please does not mean 'now you can't say no.'

I often tell my students this: 'Think about what instruction you regularly give others that in fact really only benefits you?'

If we step back and think about it before we give an instruction in future and ask ourselves one question; 'Is this for the benefit of everyone? Or the benefit of the other person? Or is it only for my comfort and convenience?' Then we will be closer to the difference between allowing and bossing. Disallowing brings with it definite negative consequences which are very often just not worth it. We may think that disallowing gives us power, but in fact it robs our power. If people violate your space and your boundaries and you don't get upset, but instead look at them with amazement, they are less likely to do it again.

A leader gives orders all the time, but the orders are for the benefit of everyone and/or for the benefit of the company/situation. When we become bossy and arbitrary, people get resentful - including and especially children and spouses. What happens then is we find it's like pulling teeth trying to get cooperation - and we blame them.

Some of us get very good at manipulating and we manage to convince people that what we want is in their best interests. One thing is certain, if you are in the role of bossing, you will also be in the role of fighting, and it will be either the cold, silent war of avoidance, or the verbose war of accusations. You'll still spend half your life either angry or lonely. Bossy people stir up a lot of negative feelings in the people they boss around. Most bossy people do not know just how bossy they are. If you want to know whether you are bossy or not, ask the following question to those who know you well:

'I think I can be bossy at times. Am I?'

Do not react to their answer because if you do, they won't tell you the truth in future. You have to 'allow' people to tell you the truth, and no matter how much it hurts or shocks you, you have to say, 'Thank you for telling me'. If you want the truth in future, then don't give people negative consequences for telling you it.

Dignity and respect

If I want to get cooperation from someone and get them to do something, I need to take the time to explain why it is in their (or everyone's) best interests and, if what I'm saying is true, they may well buy into it. If they buy into it, they will take responsibility for it and willingly do it without being policed. If I then still police them, I am saying, 'I don't believe you are willing' or 'I don't believe you are capable'. I'm indirectly accusing them of suffering either lack of ability, or lack of integrity. I will effectively have offended them and violated the trust. That may cause them to withdraw their commitment.

We get the best cooperation from people when we give them dignity and respect; when we don't make the whole thing too personal, when we don't hold them hostage or ransom emotionally, when we allow them to choose to do it willingly, when we offer a fair exchange, when we share the responsibilities, when we each have a say as to who gets which bit of the job, when we offer to help each other only when asked, when we allow people to learn from their own mistakes. Then we work far more peacefully with others. When we expect the best and allow for a margin of error, we get a far better result.

There is one exception here, and that is if you are a manager in a work situation. In that case you are being paid to boss people around, to dominate and to manipulate, but you can still do it artfully and respectfully. When that is the case, it is best to explain to the staff that this is your job and that you are also answering to a boss who does the same with you, and expects it of you. They will understand if you are honest about it, especially if you joke about it. It is vital to also give them praise, thanks and recognition too to balance it. If you only boss, dominate and manipulate, then they will either resent you or they will become stressed. If your behaviour affects their performance negatively, the consequences will fall on you. If you are not being hired and paid to manage people, then don't take it upon yourself to manage people.

But I know I'm right!

Many years ago I used to know I was right, and I knew the right way, and I knew it with every fibre of my being, and one day someone said to me, "It's funny how the world has managed to produce billions of humans and have them live whole lives without you showing them the way." That made me feel very embarrassed and I asked myself some serious

92

questions. Ordinary, intelligent people argue or disagree with me. That's amazing. Why? Is it really because everyone else is wrong, gets things wrong or can't understand? Were so many people brought up badly? I didn't like my own upbringing that much, so how do I get to assume my way is so right? Am I really wiser than other ordinary, intelligent people? If so, how did I magically get to be that way? Or could it be that I feel 'less' when I'm wrong? If I defend my position because I'm afraid of being wrong (my own intrinsic sense of value), maybe they are too (their intrinsic sense of value). Who knows who is right? Surely if something works, then it's right.

Then I asked myself, why does anyone have to be wrong? Why can't we just be different? Surely there can be more than one point of view, more than one way of seeing things, more than one correct way, more than one good, workable list of values and rules? People have existed for millennia without you or I explaining to them the right way. Since the human race has survived, there must evidently be thousands of ways to be in the world. It made sense to me to notice that if some people lived happier and more successful lives than me, it must mean that some ways are better than the ones I thought were the one right way.

Objective reality

We think that reality is objective, but it seldom is. To humans discussing it, it can usually only be subjective because it is the truth only according to our own unique, personal experience and beliefs about it. We all have very different ideas about what reality is. So often we think that we are objective, therefore everyone who disagrees with us is off track. They are not off track, they merely have a different reality. The way they see and interpret the world is

93

different. The things they hold as important are different. The things they notice and the things they don't notice are different. Their ideas, beliefs and choices are different. In fact everybody is different from everyone else, so experience must be subjective and not objective. If it were objective, then we'd all agree on all things.

If I see a mother giving her child a smack in the supermarket I may think, 'What a nasty mother.' Someone else may think, 'I'm glad to see some people control their children in supermarkets.' Another may think, 'How embarrassing for that poor kid.' There must be a hundred different ways that a hundred different people could interpret that one incident. Whatever happens to us or around us has absolutely no value or meaning other than the value or meaning we attach to it. What we hold in our thoughts is not the event itself, but our interpretation of it.

We take our deep, underlying assumptions for granted, and seldom even realise they are there. Some people find it extremely difficult to even imagine that someone else has a different reality, let alone try to understand it. Most people's compulsion is to argue for their own reality, or look for similarities and use that as a basis to believe we are all the same.

We can't even get the eyewitnesses of a car accident to agree upon the facts and finer details of what happened, unless they have discussed it amongst themselves immediately after the crash at the scene. This discussing helps them to 'agree'. People have this uncanny urge to agree. For some reason, having a different reality seems to make people feel insecure. Most of us were brought up to believe that someone must be confused or lying if the stories don't tally exactly. This belief is a fallacy because no stories ever tally exactly, even after we've adjusted what we initially thought to match a shared reality.

It is not unusual for a person to imagine that their credibility is at stake if another person says they are wrong, especially when they are verbalising 'obvious facts'. People begin to argue for their personal value, feeling compelled to be right - and see the other as wrong - because they imagine that if the other person is right, that makes them wrong (or stupid, confused, off track or telling lies). People usually eventually choose to agree on at least some of 'the facts', because of the discomfort or trauma of confrontation or of being 'wrong'. We often settle for a peaceful compromise - outwardly conforming, inwardly complacent. But it doesn't have to be this way.

A bigger problem comes into play when two stubborn, ego-bound people try to 'agree' upon the facts, but neither one is prepared to give an inch. The comparison of facts deteriorates into a verbal war zone with each accusing the other of being stupid, blind or crazy, and feeling absolutely convinced that the other is wrong and must at all costs be proved wrong and put right. The more stubborn they are, the angrier or more frustrated they get as they each contribute generously to the creating of hostile negative energy. Each blames the other for making them so mad.

It is perfectly possible for two normal, intelligent, sane, individuals to look at exactly the same thing, completely disagree, and yet both be right. This is because we are all looking at everything through our own, unique glasses of experience, interpretation and understanding. What we see has absolutely no value other than the value we place on it, the value we believe it has, what we believe we have seen, and what we think it means. What we say has absolutely no value either, other than what we mean by what we say, and what the other took our words to mean.

Far more important is the effect our words create. Our lives are a result of how we think, speak and behave. There is always some way to behave or some set of words to say that would get us the result we actually want. 'Right' or 'wrong' has little to do with it. The actual results we get are what counts. The quality of our lives and our relationships are the important things. Being far-sighted instead of short-sighted and remembering that the other person really actually believes they are right will help us choose our response wisely enough to create the next moment as we want to have it. The past is gone, but the next moment is ours to shape any way we want.

So, both our reality and the reality of the other person has a strong influence on our communication of objective reality with another. If we can be happy to allow someone else to completely disagree with us, and not be compelled to put them straight, we can learn a huge amount. If we can let them disagree and not feel bad in any way, we do ourselves a huge favour. We can gain their opinion plus have our own opinion and then have two opinions. It could be fascinating and not at all frustrating. It could be quite educational.

We can open our minds a little and listen with intent to understand rather than intent to reply. Bear in mind that the other person is a completely different individual with completely different paradigms, a totally different reality and a different map of the world. Just be fascinated, not irritated. Whether the other person believes you or accepts you or not is just as unimportant as the 'facts' of the case. It all boils down to human relationships and not the 'objective reality' we are arguing for. Being free, happy and at peace is the main thing. I forget who first coined this excellent phrase, 'what you think of me is none of my business'.

How can it hurt to allow others to be right in their own eyes? There are plenty of responses we can choose that help us keep our sanity when someone's words run contrary to our map of the world. Here are a few suggestions:

- Thank you for showing me your point of view.
- Thank you for helping me see another perspective.
- I'm fascinated at how we can both see the same thing so completely differently.
- Please help me see how you came to that conclusion/ decision/ understanding/ etc. Not because I intend to change my view to match yours, not because I need evidence to prove you wrong, but because it is fascinating to me to see how different people 'see' things so differently from one another.

Allowing others does not mean I have to change my own point of view. It does not mean I have given in. I don't have to force my point of view on them and I don't have to tell them that they are wrong. I don't have to change and they don't have to change. I merely allow them to have a point of view that is different from mine, and just for fun, I can imagine what life would look like to me if I believed what they do.

Some people might think doing this makes them a doormat, but it doesn't. Being a doormat happens when we do not allow ourselves. Doormats give all their power away, afraid to stand up for themselves, wanting to please others, even at their own expense. They think they have to accept someone else's point of view in place of their own, or at least they pretend to out of a fear. They think that allowing another to be right means they have to give up or give in and lose.

People often don't realize that they can keep their own opinions, pride and dignity regardless, and they don't even have to tell anyone that they hold a different view if they don't want others to know that. You can let people know you see it differently, or you can keep that information to yourself. It doesn't matter. Do what seems the wisest and best choice for the situation.

Once you see what it is to give others the space, the dignity and respect to believe whatever they want, you will automatically see what it means to give it to yourself. The revelation comes through simultaneously. Allowing others without changing yourself will show you that you are also allowed to be yourself - even if that annoys others.

I'm a doormat lying here
for you to wipe your feet.
I'll do anything you say
because I am so sweet.

People know I can't say no,
they use me all the time.
And when they say "You're looking sad,"
I tell them "No, I'm fine"

I don't want to be getting
anything I don't deserve,
and so I ask for nothing cause,
I haven't got the nerve.

Because I'm so agreeable
I don't want to impose.
I'm kind, obliging, helpful,
I hope everybody knows.

by Terri Ann Laws

Doormats need to learn to treat themselves with respect and give themselves the right to say no. If I get a flood of awful emotions when people say 'no' to me (rejection), and I get a flood of awful emotions when I want to say 'no' to them (fear), I've got a 'No is a no no.' problem. Every time I say yes to them, I feel I have lost something, or I feel they owe me or I feel they have used me, and I keep the score. Every time I say no to them, I feel guilty. That's not dignity and respect, that's barter and trade. That's not fair give and take, it's hostage and ransom. If you've tried it, you've seen it doesn't work.

Some people live 'through' others. They get their opinions, values, rules and everything else from those they attach themselves to. They don't make clear distinctions of where they end and the world begins. They get upset if people park in front of their house, even though they know perfectly well that the road outside their house is not their property and is the public domain available to any road user. Some feel their own feelings in response to what someone close to them is doing. They feel included in or responsible for or embarrassed by someone else's behaviour. Take this example:

Let's pretend that I am 'attached' to you in this way (pretend I am your partner or friend or your sister or something). You and I go to a local restaurant down the road that has live music. Halfway through our meal the musician plays a happy sing-a-long song. You know the words, you're in an excellent good mood, so you stand up, raise your arms and start singing out loud. I grab your sleeve and hiss, "Shhhh! Shut up!!! Sit down!!! You'll make a spectacle of yourself. You are embarrassing me!" What is the thinking behind this response of mine? What am I really saying? Am I saying:

- ..I don't have the courage to express myself, and so I don't want you to have the courage either?
- ..I don't know where you end and I begin, so I feel like I am doing things when you do them?
- ..My inner feeling tells me to control myself. If I have to control myself then you must control yourself too?
- ..I'm getting my sense of self worth (value) from you, so if you don't remain predictable, calm and sedate, I won't have any self worth (value)?
- ..I'm hiding behind you. If you jump up and down, someone will see me?
- ..I'm afraid of attention. When you attract attention, I feel like the attention is on me?
- ..I'm not an independent person, I'm a part of you. So whatever you do, people will accuse me of doing, and I don't want to be guilty of that particular behaviour?
- ..I want absolute control over you. You are not allowed to be spontaneous or have fun without my consent. I will only give you consent when I feel comfortable with it?
- ..We need permission from all these other people if we want to relax and be ourselves?
- ..Other people's opinion of us is more important than what we think of ourselves. We dare not do anything or have any fun if there is the slightest risk of these strangers having a bad opinion of us?

- ..I am not able to let go of my childhood training. I feel like all these other people here are grownups, but we are children. We're supposed to sit quietly and be good or we'll be in trouble?

- ..Everybody here is more important than we are. We need to bow low subserviently and politely in case we offend any one of them?

See how ridiculous it sounds when I put it this way? If we think about what we are really saying by implication as we disallow people, we may get closer to an understanding of allowing. This applies to our kids as well. Sometimes we put all our own fears, insecurities and complexes on to our children without even realizing we are doing it. We stifle their spontaneity when we feel shy or insecure. We keep them at heel when we feel nervous.

Try doing an internal memory check to see if you have times and places in your life where you delete the boundaries between you and someone else in this way. Some parents delete the boundaries between themselves and their children not realizing that the consequences make it possible to hurt themselves even more than they hurt the child. It reaffirms and practices our own fears and insecurities, and more importantly, it puts our fears and insecurities into our children. This is not only re-living our fears and insecurities through our children, it is also teaching the children to have them as well.

Everyone on earth has a God given right to be themselves, and people who are different are usually liked more for it, not liked less for it. If you don't feel OK about allowing others to be different, investigate why.

If you let people be whoever it is they are without judging them, you will slowly learn to let yourself be whoever it is you are without judging yourself. As you learn to allow others, so will you learn to allow yourself. Once you allow yourself, you'll be able to have more of a good time and enjoy life more. Others will be able to relax with you, feel more comfortable, and actually love you and trust you a lot more too.

In the role of leadership we obviously have to often tell people what to do and often not allow everyone to do whatever they whatever they want, so this brings up the question: when do we use leadership, and when do we use allowing? The answer to that is: it's a value judgement. Question your motives. Check if you have the authority and permission. Question yourself to assess and make sure you are not reflecting your fears, insecurities and complexes on to others. Make sure you are not forcing others to do things your way just for the sake of maintaining control. Ask yourself if the situation actually requires you to tell people what to do. Do you have the permission from the hearts of those you're leading to be their leader? Do some kind of reality check and then you won't go far wrong.

Obviously if you have been appointed as the leader/manager you'll be doing a lot more organizing and controlling than otherwise. However, you'll get far better cooperation from those you are leading/managing if you are sensitive and allowing whenever possible as well. Be strong, be free, be spontaneous and be happy. Most of all, let others live free as well.

Though I'm instructed the part I'm to play
In the nicest, 'requesting' and friendliest way,
The feeling I have at the end of the day
Is 'I really had something important to say'

Including all others is such a gem,
It brings out committed devotion in them.
But if you just tell them how it should be
It brings out 'the duty expected of me.'

Why see advice and opinions and views
As objections, rejections or critical news.
In fact they are helpful and given in love,
It shows a keen interest, not a keen shove.

Lots of the spirit and joy in the air
Is dampened by thoughts of 'who, why and fair'
All the ideas in each person's head
Remain, as they're thinking 'We should have instead...'

If the event should turn out all wrong,
Where does the blame then really belong?
But everyone's being so polite and so nice,
You don't want to look at the actual price.

If all the opinions are valued and used,
And no one's opinion is flatly refused,

And everyone fully agrees to the plan,
We'll all work together as best as we can.

Then if the event should turn out all wrong,
No one is blaming. Together we're strong.
There's no disappointment, we all make a plan.
We're standing together like one happy clan.

by Terri Ann Laws

So stop bossing and let us all plan things together!

Creating

We create our own destiny, our own reality

A wealthy businessman came into financial troubles. Things went from bad to worse. In a desperate attempt to salvage the situation, he made a very unwise choice. The results left him penniless. His house, his car, his furniture and everything he owned was taken away from him, leaving him penniless and homeless with nothing. What do you think he did? What do you think a man in this situation usually does?

Did he become a tramp or a beggar? Did he look for a home in the shelter or camp amongst the homeless who, like him, have nothing? Did he sign up for benefit or get food stamps? No! People who 'think' rich, just don't make those kinds of choices, even when they have absolutely no money. He struggled along staying with friends and family while he searched frantically for a job or a business opportunity to make himself a living. He was single- minded in his purpose. He had every intention of remaining in his comfort zone of plenty. Within three months, he had rented a house, was self-supporting again, with a job, a car and furniture. It wasn't much, but it was a start. No way in the world would he settle for less than an acceptable lifestyle.

He was well on his way to creating life as he knew it, wanted it and expected it to be. He recreated his own reality according to what he thought he was, according to what he thought he deserved, according to where he thought he belonged. He saw his plight of poverty as extremely temporary. He had no intention of getting used to having nothing. He decided that he was a rich man who temporarily had nothing. For that reason, it wasn't too long

106

before he was a rich man again. The second time he became rich, he became three times richer. It took him less than half the time it took the first time, and he put loads more protections in place to secure his wealth.

A humble, poor man from a very shabby neighbourhood won £900, 000 at the casino. He was totally ecstatic. He squandered it lavishly within six months. He bought all the things he could never before afford. He generously spoiled all his friends and family. He lived like a king denying himself nothing until every penny was spent.

During the following six months, he sold all the things he had bought, one by one, and spent the money trying to maintain the 'good life' he had enjoyed during the previous six months. Within a year he was again a humble, poor man in a very shabby neighbourhood with nothing but memories, some bitter, some exciting, and a great story to share with all his friends and family for life. He didn't improve his lot in life, because he still saw himself as a lowly, poor man who once got lucky.

It is we ourselves who have decided where we fit in, where we belong. We are creating our own reality, our own destiny, and our own life. Some scientists now believe we even create our own body. Once we realize this, we can decide where we would rather feel comfortable. We can begin creating a very different reality if we want to. One small step at a time, we can move towards the kind of life and surroundings we want to have as our own. Creating begins in the mind, and the life we create every day in our minds with our consistent thoughts, beliefs and 'inner movies' is the life we create in the real world.

The book *Think And Grow Rich* by Napoleon Hill is reputed to have created more millionaires than any other source in history. Yet the 'secret' didn't jump out at me the first time I read the book as Napoleon promised. It didn't even jump out at me the second time I read the book. Some years went by before I read the book for the third time, and then it hit me like a ton of bricks and I laughed and laughed in utter amazement and delight at how my own limiting beliefs had hid the secret from me so well for all those years.

You are a creator. You have creative talents. Maybe in cooking, arts, music, maths, business, gardens, friendships, decor, atmosphere, money... there are thousands of possibilities.

We are creating all the time. What do we create? A meal, a conversation, an idea, an atmosphere, relationships, a home, an appearance, friendships, our career and all kinds of things. We also create negative things like arguments, dismal imaginings of what might happen, or perhaps debt. Whether we are deliberately and consciously creating or not, we are nevertheless creating as we go about our day. Even in a coma we are creating ... work for others.

The idea is to become aware of what we are creating so that we can deliberately create what we do want, and stop accidentally creating what we don't want. A person who is convinced that he is upper class will never settle for lower class - regardless of what life throws at him. A person who is convinced he is of the lower class will feel totally inferior in the upper class even if he has a university degree and wins a few million pounds. We decide what our reality is, and that decision causes us to continuously create our reality. Our reality exists in our beliefs. We can change all that. We can change our mental picture. We can change our identity and our entire life.

The day we are born we begin making the mental maps that form our reality. Every experience we have, everything we hear or see or touch or feel inside, we chalk up according to our own unique interpretation of what it means. We begin to do this even before we have language, even before we get words from others. We formulate opinions, we think, say, feel and do, and then draw conclusions based on the reactions or responses or consequences we witness or suffer. This becomes the 'truth', the 'facts' (reality), to us. No two of us look at life and see the same picture, because we all draw our own unique conclusions about everything. We all have our own original ideas of what those conclusions mean – and about what is going to happen next.

We do not see the world as it is, we see the world as we are, or as we have been conditioned to see it. We set out and do, be or say according to our interpretations and understandings. When we open our mouths to describe the world, we only describe ourselves. People know who we are by what we do and say.

Our words and actions flow from our thoughts and beliefs. Our words and actions shape and create our relationships. The way others see us and the way we see ourselves is what opens or closes doors. We create our dreams, plans, security, relationships and everything else based on what we believe to be true. Based on what we think we ought to do, have to do, must do, shouldn't do or can't do. We go out and get all the things, ideas, information, people, tools, possessions, whatever we choose or think we need, and we put together a life. We make all those choices. We decide what should or should not happen.

Wishing for something reaffirms the fact that you don't have it. The belief that you don't have it keeps the equilibrium. It's no use wishing for peace in your home, you need to create peace in your home. It's no use hoping your life will be easy, you have to create an easy life. Whatever you want, create the circumstances that are conducive to it. Create all the necessary things that will lead up to it. Create friendships with people who can advise you or help you get there. Create good business relationships so that when the time is right you can get credit or start up your own enterprise. Create safety nets to fall into so that you can take chances. Create a strong character that cannot be threatened. Create a fun personality that will be attractive to people. Study, learn, grow and create yourself, create your relationships and create the life you want.

Take one small step at a time and learn to deliberately create your own circumstances, your own destiny. Learn to make things happen the way you want them to. Start by creating one small thing every day: a pretty flower arrangement, a drawing, a new friendship, a new way of walking, a new tone of voice, a new way of dealing with an old problem, anything just for practice. If something in your life isn't working, try creating something else by doing something differently or doing something else instead.

Try on someone else's beliefs and see what the world would look like if you believed that too. Become more aware of the fact that you can deliberately create your experiences and circumstances. Try things more than once or twice to see if practice improves the outcome. Wherever you are,

110

whoever you are, is a result of all the choices you made all those yesterdays. You created the life that you have and you created the person you are. You may have been the using raw materials that were handed down to you, but you have the creative ability to change your life.

Questions to ask yourself

- How did I create this reality I find myself in?
- What other choices did I have that I thought I couldn't/shouldn't take?
- What was I thinking? What am I still thinking?
- What deep internal beliefs (facts, truths, realities) am I holding on to?
- What activities do I spend time doing?
- What activities do I avoid doing?
- What are the things I judge wrong or impossible or unwise or stupid?
- What must I stop doing or start doing to change things?
- How do I see the world that I find myself in?
- How do I see the people I have surrounded myself with?
- Is this the reality that I want?
- Do I know what I really want?
- What my potential is?
- How much of my reality am I aware of creating myself?
- How much of my reality do I feel has been created for me? Why? What factors did I think were beyond my control?
- What emotional states do I find myself in most of the time?

- How are those states affecting what I will and won't do?
- What words and voice tones in my repertoire create the most problems for me?
- What words and behaviours from me bring out the best in others?
- How much responsibility am I taking for what I create?

You yourself are a unique creation of nature. You have the capacity, the ability and the responsibility to deliberately create, and doing so greatly improves your life. It makes you feel powerful and capable. It actually makes you become powerful and capable. It gives life meaning and excitement. It helps you become a doer - instead of only a talker or wishful dreamer. Creativity replaces negative thinking with positive action.

An ancient bushman saying:

"There are three types of people:
Those who make things happen, those who watch things
happen, and those who wonder what happened."

Here is an example. It really actually is just this simple. Try it. What have you got to lose?

Creating my own reality, starting with my own business

Let's say I want to create my own decorating business. I already have the talent and hundreds of decorating magazines for ideas and inspiration. What do I still need?

- A car. I can't collect that, I don't have the money, so I have to attract it. (see below and the chapter on 'Attracting')
- An attractive 'people personality'. I can't collect that either, I have to learn it. I can also attract it.
- Customers. Those I can collect through advertising.
- Suppliers. Those I can collect through their advertising.
- An attractive catalogue to show my customers. That I can create by researching the latest trends and using pictures cut out of magazines.
- A pricing structure. That I can create after collecting information from other similar businesses.

I'll start with attracting that bubbly, 'peoples person' type personality for popularity to ensure everyone helps me, and to ensure all potential customers become actual customers and to ensure I get loads of referrals.

- I start thinking about it. I daydream and imagine I have it and I fantasize myself being like that.
- I start looking around to see who has got it and who hasn't got it
- I start looking deeper at the differences between those who do and those who don't have it.
- I assimilate the information I've gathered and assess what it teaches me

- I go in search of more information, experience and examples. I discuss it with others, I ask questions, I read and do whatever research I can.
- I spend a lot of time around those who have it, watching, seeing, learning, enjoying and attracting.
- I try to see the world through their eyes, from their perspective. I try on their beliefs and values and personalities.
- I notice what they've got that I lack, and determine to add that to me.
- I start practising saying the things they say, the way they say them, and doing the things they do the way they do them.
- Once I think I'm getting the hang of it, I take a good long look at myself. I let others give me feedback. I ask for help and opinions. I look to see if I'm getting all of it right yet.
- I imagine myself being fully like that all the time and amplify the wonderful feelings it gives me inside.
- If not, I try again, and again, and again, until I do get it right in all ways. I practise being exactly like the role models I have selected, then I practise again in the real world.

Lo and behold, laughter is contagious, I get it right. I've attracted the personality I needed.

Now I get to work on attracting the car. How do I attract a car?

- I start thinking about a car, day and night.
- I start frequenting garages and second-hand car shops and I look at all the cars available.
- I see what each one feels like.
- I imagine myself owning them.
- I sit in them, examine them, and get to know what I like.
- I start taking cars on test drives, pretending I own the one I'm test driving.
- I evaluate all options, new ones, second-hand ones, old crocks, anything and everything to decide my best option.
- I leave no stone unturned.
- I go see finance companies and collect quotes on various options and car deals.
- I read the 'motor' sections of every newspaper and magazine.
- I tell everyone I know that I urgently need a car to start my own business, yet I don't have the money.
- I listen to all the advice and suggestions - without concentrating on why they won't work, but rather concentrate on how they might work.
- I keep assimilating the information I've gathered, and I keep collecting more.
- I get more and more excited about the car I'm going to buy.
- I get more and more specific about the exact car that I need or want.
- I decide the age (new or old), the make, the features, the price, the financing, everything.
- Now I start plotting ways to get it.

115

- By now I have become single-mindedly, absolutely determined to get it, and in my mind I already have it.
- With my intense focused attention and networking I start running into the inevitable coincidences and luck.
- People give me information, leads, help and possibly even money, or a good loan, or perhaps someone even gives me the car!

Lo and behold, by hook or by crook, I get the car.

In this 'decorating business' example, you can see how you can aim any business or any dream you like. It all begins in the mind. If you can see yourself having what you want, living the life you want, and if you believe that you can get it, you will. If you realize that it is up to you to create the life you want, the circumstances you want, then you'll start doing just that. It is no one else's job to get you what you want and need. It is your job, and it is easier than you think. Everything man ever created first began with a thought. Think it is easy and it is, it really is.

Even your relationships with all the people you know first began with a thought about them when you first saw or heard them, and that thought was based on a belief. Your words and actions came from your thoughts and beliefs and that is the 'you' they came to know and respond to. People are the way they are to you because of the way you are. Change your thoughts and beliefs and you'll create very different relationships. The relationships you have will change drastically if you change. The circumstances you find yourself in will change drastically if you change. Create your relationships and create your life – on purpose and not by

116

default. Your relationships will help you tremendously in creating your life the way you want it to be.

You are creating your life in every second of your existence, and as soon as you realize that, you can start creating deliberately and on purpose and no longer create by default.

'Whatever the mind of man can conceive and believe he can achieve' W Clement Stone

'You'll see it when you believe it'' Wayne Dyre

Guilt

Guilt causes great pain and is very destructive. It can affect a person in any number of ways, such as the following:

- Becoming defensive and reactive.
- A drop in self-esteem. Feeling worthless.
- Justifying oneself all the time.
- Guilt haunts thoughts and keeps them negative.
- Looking for blame, shame and guilt in others.
- Believing we don't deserve.
- Avoiding certain things, places or people.
- Hampering personal growth.
- Suffering terrible emotional pain.
- Feeling fear, depressed and wanting to withdraw.
- Getting physically ill.
- Becoming depressed
- Sleep problems.

There are two types of guilt. One comes from knowing we did something wrong, the other hangs over us and we don't know why or where it's coming from. We'll start with the first one.

It is very important to take careful stock of mistakes from a disassociated, detached and objective viewpoint, and to separate yourself from all bad feelings associated with the mistake. Do a brief analysis as to how the mistake happened and whether it could be avoided in the future. Learn as much as possible from it to render the experience useful instead of only all bad, and be pleased you learned a valuable lesson.

We must forgive ourselves and allow ourselves to be human. Would you wish terrible suffering and guilt on your best friend if he/she did something they felt was really wrong and felt really bad about? Of course not! You would surely comfort them and help them get over it. That's what you should do for yourself. Be your own best friend, take your own hand and help yourself through it. Running 'if only ...' scenarios over and over in your mind will torture you without any useful benefit. Remember as well that trying to justify the thing you did wrong keeps you stuck with the guilt.

It would be fantastic if we could turn back the clock and do things differently, but that is not going to happen, so learn from mistakes, forgive yourself and get over it as quickly as you can, knowing you'll never make the same mistake again. Recovery requires huge amounts of courage, self nurture and self-honesty. I know it can be so hard sometimes, but it is absolutely necessary if you want to be free and have inner peace.

Taking the blame

It is important not to cast the blame elsewhere and try to get away from responsibility that way. Of course anyone can find or create reasons why it's actually the other person's fault, for example rewinding to some previous incident, or looking for a fault in the other person's character or assuming they should have done something differently. Anyone can do that. But the trouble is if it's their fault, then there is absolutely no reason for you to change or say sorry, and then there is nothing for you to benefit, learn or grow from. Then you might easily find the guilt goes underground and manifests as unwanted symptoms somewhere else in your life. Unconscious (underground) guilt often grows things like depression, insomnia, panic attacks and anxiety.

If I've done something wrong, I have a choice: I can blame something or someone else and keep suffering, or blame myself so that it becomes my responsibility and I can look for ways to grow from it and/or fix it. If it's my fault, I can do something about it, learn something from it and make different choices in future. If it's their fault, I'm helpless. Which would you rather be: guilty and capable of fixing it and growing from it, or innocent and helpless and paralysed with uncomfortable feelings lurking inside you forever? Most people have enormous respect for a person who takes the blame, especially if they take it with strength and power, standing tall and making eye contact.

What to do with blame once you've taken it (taken responsibility)

I can take the blame and fix it, or take the blame and beat myself up with it, wallowing in self-hatred, self-pity, guilt and depression. This second choice is totally destructive. It is a complete indulgence in woe and self-pity and can become a psychological, neurotic disorder. There is no point in taking the blame for any reason other than to fix it. It's simple: if we don't take the blame, we remain in a victim mentality. If we do take the blame, we can learn something, we can do something about it and avoid similar problems in future. Taking the blame makes you a much bigger person, and it makes other people safer with you. It takes courage to openly and honestly say, 'I did wrong there', but it is the only way to become totally free, because having admitted it, it can be released and let go of. Don't take the blame to feel terrible and guilty; take the blame to feel strong and empowered and to increase your choices.

Always we must take the blame,
But never cling to guilt and shame,
As we learn we grow, we gain,
Abundant joy comes after pain.

by Terri Ann Laws

Where does guilt come from?

It comes from conscience, and having a conscience means you are a good person. Your conscience just might need some updating. We have two distinct, different consciences - the *induced conscience* or *authoritarian conscience*, and the *natural conscience*.

The induced conscience is installed into us when we are small by the people who raise us and influence us; those who had authority or power over us - parents, teachers, church authorities for example who tell us what is right and wrong according to their beliefs. They instilled the relevant bad or fearful feelings in us to ensure we thought, felt and behaved as they deemed appropriate. For example, they may have told us that it is selfish to say no; it is greedy to ask for a second helping; and it is inconsiderate to play on Saturday afternoons if your parents are trying to sleep. You may have been told that if you can't say something nice, don't say anything at all; that, if you are a Catholic, it's a sin to eat meat on Good Friday; if you are a Jew you shouldn't eat pork. You may be told that big boys don't cry; it is rude to stare at people; don't tell lies; always be fair and share equally and it's very bad to love money. There are thousands and thousands of examples, and you'll have your own selection, I'm sure.

Also included in 'induced conscience' are the statements, insults and accusations we received from authority figures when we were children. Many of us spend most of our adult life trying to prove those adults wrong - sometimes long after that adult has died! If your father kept telling you that you were irresponsible, you may spend your entire adult life trying to prove to others that you are not.

The induced conscience is the authoritarian conscience. It is often void of common sense, often arbitrary and very often completely untrue or unrealistic. Yet it is a powerful conscience. Many people never transcend it. They feel guilty when they violate it. Some feel guilty even questioning it. They have completely bought into it and accepted this conscience as their own inner conscience. They are utterly convinced that these beliefs they hold are definite facts and actually constitute the genuine right and wrong or good and bad of human behaviours.

People can generate a massive amount of guilt every time they violate these induced principles, beliefs or values that are so ingrained. Some of these principles, beliefs or values are almost impossible not to violate – especially some of the religious ones. They are contrary to normal human thinking, feeling and behaviour. Just being humans means we have to sin. For example: 'Don't have evil thoughts! Thinking about the opposite sex in a sexual way is evil!' Now, how on earth can a normal human being not violate that at some point in his/her life? No human being is capable of keeping sexual thoughts out of their minds from birth till death.

Another one is, 'Never tell a lie!' Situations arise now and then where the truth would deeply hurt someone or cause more harm than good. There are times when a person who has power, but has no right to the information they are demanding from you, or no right to have asked the question they're asking you, demands information or answers from you. In this case, one might be cornered to lie because the consequences of telling the truth are unacceptable or destructive or disloyal to someone else. How can one avoid this? A lot of these induced rules are impossible to honour for life, and sooner or later, being human will force you to violate them, and then the consequential guilt arises.

The other conscience we have is the Natural conscience. This is our own choice and feelings telling us that something is good or bad based on our own understanding, common sense, logic and good judgement. The more we question our induced conscience and weigh it up against reality, common sense and logic, the more our natural conscience will grow. The more we learn the human dynamic, the less we will be vulnerable to our authoritarian induced conscience and the consequential guilt that it generates.

Some sales people are trained to make customers feel guilty on purpose to bully them into buying. Common tricks are accusing the poor customer of wrong doing such as, 'I have just spent so much time with you teaching you about this product and you've been wasting my time all along, leading me to believe you were interested'. 'How can you let me down now? Why didn't you tell me sooner you weren't interested.' Another one that's popular with insurance salesmen is, 'Are you going to leave your family vulnerable with no one to take care of them and no one to pay the bills or feed them if you suddenly die?'

Some couples use guilt to control each other and some parents use guilt to control their children and to get compliance, and some friends use guilt to get more attention and to get what they want. As long as we don't examine all the things that cause us to feel guilty, and take a good hard look at them, we remain vulnerable to being manipulated.

Values and actions.

Another thing that can cause guilt is deciding we have certain values or principles, and then not behaving in accordance with them. For example, putting a huge value on generosity and giving, but then feeling reluctant to actually part with money and give to others. Valuing gentleness and polite behaviour and then getting angry and behaving harshly, or valuing honesty and then telling lies. Valuing fitness but never doing exercise, or highly valuing people who are widely read but never reading a book. We sense the duplicity between what we believe in and what we actually practise, so we feel guilty. Violations of our own principles and values can leave us feeling inadequate and guilty.

To rectify the problem, clarify your values and principles and line them up with your actual practices, or change your practices. Do not live at variance with your values and principles. Change either one or the other so that you are living true to yourself. (See Values)

Obedience and disobedience

Disobedience is usually nothing more than obedience to something else. If I am obeying society's expectations of me, I could be disobeying my expectations of myself. If a teenager is obeying his parents he might be disobeying the expectations and norms of his peers and friends. If the two ever clash, we have to make a value judgement. We have to decide what's the right thing to do based on our own ideas of right and wrong. If I make my choice out of fear, subservience, induced conscience or something else not true to myself, I may regret it and suffer guilt. Obedience to one thing often requires disobedience to something else. Be true to yourself and then you can say 'no' without feeling guilty.

For example, let's say society expects me to give to the poor. I personally feel that we insult people and keep them thinking they are helpless and 'less than' when we hand out charity for nothing. So one day a starving, scrawny, female beggar with a baby on her hip comes to my door when I have friends over. I tell her to clean out the flowerbeds for money and food. Then I look at my friends. I see their shocked faces. Obviously they feel I should help the poor woman for nothing. I'm torn between society's expectations of me and my own inner conscience. I can then buy into their conscience, doubt myself and feel guilty.

Live in harmony and congruence within yourself and become clear about who and what you are, and who and what you want to be obedient to. Know your reasons why you feel as you do, and behave in alignment with what you believe is right. Have the courage to be true to your convictions, and then you'll escape the trap of society's pressures on you to behave as they feel rather than as you know is right.

The child in trouble and child causing trouble.

I had a client who suffered terrible guilt. She would feel guilty for nothing. The slightest thing would trigger it, and no amount of rational thinking would help her to stop feeling it. If she asserted herself appropriately, she'd feel guilt. If she said 'no' to one of her kids, she'd feel guilt. If she said she didn't like a food someone gave her, again the guilt would come up. It was driving her nuts. After a couple of hours of chatting, she remembered that she used to get a particular child into trouble a lot at school. She was able to blame this child for anything and consequently get away with just about anything.

Then she admitted she'd done the same thing to her little brother. She found she was good at it. At one point she even began stealing because she was able to accuse some innocent person and get away with it. We soon realised the link, and it seemed obvious why she now suffered so much guilt over nothing at all. She'd long forgotten these childhood incidents, but the incidents had not forgotten her. After helping this client, the realisations helped me to understand other clients I've had who suffer guilt - guilt they cannot explain, because they have long forgotten the original situations.

Buried deeply in the recesses of their minds, under thick blankets of denial, lie the painful memories of watching an innocent child crying in despair from undeserved punishment, insults, rejection, thrashings, rebuke or whatever. The victim often suffers less long-term damage than the child who was guilty. Hidden guilt can in some cases fester forever.

From my many years of experience as a counsellor and therapist, I have become convinced that in the long run, it hurts more to have been the perpetrator than to have been the victim. Most people find it is easier to forgive others than to forgive themselves. The guilty don't always fair better when they have got away with some bad deed at someone else's expense. Temporary relief can be replaced by long-term guilt. They feel like a coward, because that is what they are. They see innocent people get into trouble. If they dislike the people they got into trouble, they may laugh and brag about it at the time, but inside they damage their character.

People who have done something (or a few things) they know are absolutely wrong can get to a stage when they can't trust people because somewhere inside they assume others could do bad things to them too. They can no longer trust themselves, and they no longer like themselves because of the deep, ugly secrets that prompt them to pretend, play games, justify their actions, lie to themselves and remain on the defensive. They find they are always looking over their shoulder, feeling suspicious, cautious and wary all the time. They don't trust anymore. The worse they feel inside, the worse they behave outside, and the worse they become as people. This affects their lives so badly, they end up getting much more 'punishment' in the long term.

You think you can convince me
with your rationalizing charm.,
You advocate your innocence,
you meant nobody harm.

I'm not prepared to argue,
I'll pretend that I agree,
Because you relish fighting and
you'll turn your wrath on me.

One thing is for certain,
you will never be my friend
because I cannot trust you.
I'll be wary to the end.

by Terri Ann Laws

Guilt is more than a bad feeling

Guilt is more than just a bad feeling inside. It is capable of causing us to wear masks, be in denial, play games and other uncomfortable side effects. If latent guilt was hiding in me somewhere, I would be less likely to want to examine myself and get to know who I really am because I'd be terrified of what I might find if I looked inside. The fear of being 'found out' would keep me hiding away from my inner self. I may have long since forgotten what I'm guilty of, or even forgotten that I have guilt, yet the fear of being 'found out' won't go away and keeps creeping out at inappropriate places and times. I might find myself feeling guilty for absolutely no explainable reason. People who flatly refuse to do a personality quiz in front of others, often have this problem

Let's face it, what goes down better socially, taking the blame or passing it on? Taking it does. We show ourselves to be far bigger as a person when we take the blame, when we know we're at fault, than when we deny it. Good leaders and managers take responsibility, thereby making everyone feel safe and protected. If we say, 'It's probably my fault' or I think I got it wrong and I apologist' we attract positive energy. Everyone feels better and, fewer people accuse us. When a wrong is out in the open, we can clearly look for ways to fix it. When it is a secret, or not admitted too, it remains unresolved.

What a paradox! Shame and guilt are reduced by taking the blame. It shows great strength and character. It makes us feel honest and brave because it is honest and brave. We clear the slate, clear the air and help others feel safe enough to take their share of the blame.

When we take the blame, we keep our power. We have no dark secrets to hide. We leave nobody outwardly friendly and inwardly angry or hating us. We have nothing to worry about later. We begin to trust ourselves more. That makes others trust us more. That makes us trust others more. The whole world becomes a safer, happier, less complicated and freer place.

Ways to take the blame

- I see you are upset. Perhaps I handled the situation wrongly. Could I try again?
- I'm sure I could have done things differently. There must be another way to do this that has less adverse consequences.
- My intention is to make you happy, and you certainly don't look happy. Could you tell me more about your feelings and expectations so that I can understand you better?
- It's probably my fault.
- I think I might have made a mistake here, can you help me fix it please?
- I think I may have expected far too much.
- I guess I totally misjudged things here, didn't I?
- Wow, I really blew that one! Will you help me get it right next time?
- For some reason I felt compelled to do that! It was mean and nasty I'm really sorry.
- It seems I've done the wrong thing! What can I learn from this?
- What was I thinking!! How did I make such a mess of that!! I deserve the national prize for stupidity!

- Oh dear, you've done it all wrong! I'm sorry, it's my fault. I should have spent more time showing you how to do it.

If we are OK about taking the blame, others will be too. There is a lot wrapped up in how we do it. If you stand tall, make strong eye contact, put a smile on your face, or a fake look of disaster, take a deep breath, add a smidgeon of humour and speak in a strong confident voice, you will save face completely, and you can take the blame bravely without everyone jumping on to you to make you the scapegoat for their mistakes.

Here are some ways not to do it:
- Trying to justify what you did. That makes people accuse you more.
- Admitting you were wrong eventually and reluctantly. That makes people resentful.
- Admitting to only part of the blame, and accusing the rest. That makes people defensive.
- Owning up with guilt, fear or inferiority all over your face. This makes everyone turn you into their scapegoat. If you want to be a victim, a lot of people will oblige you.
- Beginning with profuse apology and saying 'sorry' too much.

Openly, honestly taking full responsibility from a position of strength (as a leader), and wanting to learn something useful for the future is the way that will work best for you.

We make ourselves bigger, not smaller when we take the blame, because it takes guts, strength of character, power, confidence and leadership. Taking the blame gives us more value, it makes us feel safer and it builds huge bridges of trust, love and safety - within us and around us.

Recovery from guilt

- Examine whether the guilt is in fact yours. It could be coming from your authoritarian induced conscience, social conditioning or other people's expectations of you. If it's not yours, realize this and drop it.
- If it is yours, own it. Own up! Admit it and stop denying it or covering up.
- Never justify your wrongs in the name of other people's wrongs.
- Find the courage to say sorry and make amends, or determine to do so once you've grown strong enough. Set a date in the future and work towards it. Send a card in the post - anything - just set yourself free.
- Forgive others.
- Put the whole thing in a broader perspective.
- Clearly see what you learned from it.
- Recognise your feelings. Allow your feelings to rise for recognition. Do not fear them. Allow them to teach you something for the future.
- Say to yourself, 'I'm obviously a good person because I know that what I did was not best. If I was a bad person, I'd have no conscience'.
- Train yourself by practising in your mind how you would handle similar situations differently next time. Think of ways to get results without adverse consequences.
- Once you've sorted it out and done the above, *drop it!*

If you don't drop it, you'll reap some damaging consequences emotionally, physically and mentally. So drop it! If you don't sort it out you might not be able to drop it. It could keep on sneaking back. If you are trying to drop it but it won't go away, then find out where it's coming from and sort out the root cause. Your own inner feelings are your best guide. They are there for a reason. Your emotions are your inner guidance system.

When not to take the blame

If ever you find yourself a victim of a power hungry weakling who is abusing his or her power over you, it would be a mistake to take the blame. This type of person is not behaving fair and square. These people feel powerful when they are bringing others down to their knees. For example, people like an ego-bound, immature policeman/woman, traffic warden, theory X manager, hardball salesman or security officer. Bullying and accusing others is something they enjoy. It is a pathology.

A better approach if you want to win with these kinds of people is to make them feel special, important and valuable. Ultimately, that's what they need. That will give them the validity they seek, then they are likely to back off and be nice to you. Bullies who abuse their power usually do so because they are terrified that people won't listen to them if they were nice. They are usually very insecure people, pretending to be the opposite. In order to hold on to your power, see the whole thing as a game and the object is to win with your power in tact. Placating or patronizing them and feeding their ego will make sure you win, as long as you do it with skilful finesse.

Your inner feelings are your guide in life. Use them to show you where you need to change and grow. There is no point ignoring them because feelings don't go away when ignored. If you suffer from guilt, then do something about it because guilt is a horrible feeling and it is also destructive to both yourself and your loved ones. Once you've done everything you need to do, let it go.

Let go of guilt!

Giving to the Ungrateful

Have you ever given out of the goodness of your heart, only to be stabbed in the back or taken advantage of? There are a few good reasons why this happens.

Giving is a one-way street

Giving is always a one-way street, without exceptions, unless you have negotiated a fair exchange in advance. Then it isn't giving anymore, it's a fair exchange. It is a fatal mistake to just assume that giving is a two-way street. You've heard people say that, and it isn't true.

If ever we can say, 'After all I've done for you!!' then we know we have not loved. We have attempted to purchase, bribe or coerce. If the giving is not free then the receiver becomes our victim. We have placed them in our debt against their will.

We could think that if we have given, we deserve to receive. The problem with this is that we have then not really given at all. We have attempted to purchase, bribe or coerce. If we tell people upfront that we expect something in return, they may well choose to say 'No thanks' to receiving from us. Giving without the self-honesty of openly recognising and admitting that we expect to get something back sometime is actually loaded giving. Loaded giving is a sneaky trick that lacks integrity, even if it done unintentionally. It is seldom done calculatingly. It is more often unconscious. It comes from having deep-rooted beliefs that say, 'If you give, you will receive', and 'If you give, others then owe you', that causes the implicit expectation to get something in return, even if all you expect is recognition or friendship or good press.

Giving what we need
Another mistake some people make is giving the thing they *need the most*. Sometimes, when we need something badly, we assume we could earn it by giving it. This often has its base in religious or social teachings. The trouble with this is that you might then deplete yourself even further. You could

138

also feel the pain of 'lack' as you see others receive that which you cannot seem to get, that which you so much want. You may well feel very upset that while you are so willing to give this thing to others, no one is willing to give it to you.

This could cause you to feel drained or resentful, empty or lonely, used or unappreciated. An example of this is those who go running around willingly helping everyone else, all the while wishing someone would help them. Or listening to everyone else's problems, all the while wishing someone would listen to theirs. Or when they are really struggling financially, giving all their remaining money to the preacher and looking to God for their ten-fold returns. The returns may never come.

Giving what we want

Then there is giving the thing you *want the most*. I might give the things that I have decided are wonderful things to give, based on what I put value on and what I would love to receive. The problem with this is that it may be something that I like, but it may not be something the receiver likes or wants to receive. The receiver may be too polite to tell you.

Some examples of what the receiver might think, but would not say are:

- I'm not a touchy person, I hate being hugged.
- I prefer to go by myself. I don't want company.
- I hate your taste in clothes. Now I have to actually wear this in public too!
- I'm trying to diet. I don't appreciate you giving me high-calorie treats.

- I feel terrible when you clean up my mess. Now I feel forced to rush and clean before you come.
- Can't you just accept me as I am?
- I've got a thing against cut flowers. You love them but I hate them.
- I wish you would stop surprising me with so much coffee.
- Are you insinuating that I'm incompetent by keep taking over and doing things for
- me?

When this kind of thing happens, and the receiver of our kindness starts finding it harder and harder to fake genuine delight, we sense the 'ungratefulness', and feel we have been unappreciated or used. We feel as though we are the victim, when in fact we are the perpetrator. We have put others in a very awkward and embarrassing position. We keep lovingly and kindly giving them things they don't want to have. We have set them up to be 'ungrateful' and in the wrong, with no escape route for them anywhere.

Rescuing

Rescuing is a common cause of 'ungratefulness'. Let's say you find a person in need, which causes the rescuer in you to leap into action. You may want to help them because it feels great to give, or you feel sorry for them, or because you believe that giving means you are a caring person. Since they are 'in need' and you are 'strong', you could unwittingly establish a relationship with this person on the basis that you give and they take. The basic assumption is that the stronger, bigger one is you, and they are the weak and needy one. They would then probably begin to rely on you as a source of supply of help with things they need to do or money, or encouragement or whatever it is that you are giving them. They are so thrilled to have someone to save them at last, they come to depend on you.

How do you think they'd feel if you suddenly changed how you felt about this arrangement? You could confuse them completely. Imagine if at some stage you suddenly expected to have your turn at receiving, and expected them to take their turn at giving? You would in effect be violating the trust. You can't really expect a role-change or rules-change without fair notice, without their consent, can you? Perhaps they are in absolutely no position to change roles. Perhaps they don't want to change roles. Perhaps we should have the foresight, honesty and courage to tell needy people in the first place that at some point we'll stop giving and expect to start taking.

What the rescued seldom realizes is that the rescuer is also needy. Rescuers have reasons for rescuing. What they need in return is often one or more of the following:

- Huge amounts of gratitude.
- Huge amounts of recognition and praise (never stop thanking and praising me).
- To feel that the rescued feels thoroughly rescued.
- Love.
- Respect.
- Power.
- Acceptance.
- Good press - that the rescued tells everyone how great the rescuer is.
- That the rescued remains dependent on the rescuer (you can't cope without me).
- That the rescued becomes devoted (I don't want to cope without you).

- That the rescued feels hugely indebted (where would I be without you? I owe you so much)
- That the rescued does as much, if not more, for the rescuer simultaneously (the least you can do for me is ……….. after all I've done for you).

But how could anyone possibly admit to that? These expectations are by their very nature secret. If the receiver should even vaguely guess at an unspoken agenda, the rescuer would feel hurt, exposed, defensive and vulnerable. Yet, if we are rescuing we may easily find ourselves thinking that the receiver is in the wrong, because they have let us down by not reciprocating or responding as we believed they should. So the rescuer becomes the victim. If we have ever done this, we should stop accusing others of being ungrateful, and rather keep the blame for ourselves. The rescued cannot be responsible for our needs or expectations, and they cannot be expected to bear the burdens of our needs as rescuer.

When we give to the needy, we must never lose sight of the fact that they are needy. They might remain needy indefinitely. They may never feel able to repay. If they choose to repay, see this as a delightful unexpected gift. Feel touched by the fact alone. And then we should be careful then not to weigh up the value of their giving against the value of ours. This could hurt both them and ourselves.

Needing to receive credit or gratitude for what we've done is a weak position. It shows insecurity and a lack of understanding of what is intrinsically valuable. Others are more likely to be grateful and value us if we don't ask, expect or demand it. The ill feeling we could cause if we turn on those we have given to, could rob us of any real gratitude they may have felt. We make other people feel 'less' if we assume they are not grateful. In fact we insult them. It's better to just 'believe' they are grateful and leave it at that, whether it is true or not.

Looking for proof of their gratitude could backfire. If you don't have the personal power to rescue without expecting anything back, then don't do it. Alternatively, look at your own motives and process and be honest to the rescued about what you get out of rescuing.

All that glitters is not gold.
Not all who wander are lost.
Not all expensive things have value,
And some worth far more than they cost.

Not every act of love is loving.
Not every gift is good.
Kindness need not merit trust,
And many a must is a should.

Some things are not what they seem.
Some prayers are foolish prayed.
Some good goes on un-rewarded,
And faithful hearts have strayed.

Some have mourned and grieved the things
They're better off without.
And many a silver lining's cloud
Has made the faint heart stout.

by Terri Ann Laws

144

Embarrassment

This is hard to believe, but did you know that some people feel so embarrassed about receiving, so utterly unworthy, that they go into total denial after having received? They simply cannot face it. It hurts too much. Their low or lack of self-worth or self-esteem can't compute it. I once took a whole family in to my home when they were destitute and fed them for three months for free. Years later, when I brought it up, the receiver said, 'You never gave me a thing. What are you talking about? That never happened! You're making it up.' I was flabbergasted, shocked, hurt and confused.

Remember that. It may save you a lot of frustration and heartache one day. If this has happened to you too, don't worry - you are not going crazy. All I could do is drop it and forget it. It is not worth losing any sleep over. Remember, giving is a one-way street!

Clarify your expectations before giving.

If I do not clarify my expectations up front before giving then I only have myself to blame if things go wrong downstream. It takes huge courage to do this. If I take the easy, lazy way out and just assume my expectations are self-evident or obvious, then I must be willing to accept the consequences if later it all turns sour. If we give and do so just because it is the good and right thing to do, life itself will reward us ten-fold in a thousand ways. But if we count the cost and hold people ransom or hostage, we will always be struggling with feelings of being used, abused or taken advantage of. If giving doesn't leave you feeling wonderful, useful and needed, then take a good, hard look at yourself and your motives. Perhaps you are only giving because you yourself are starving to receive.

145

There is a very important point to add here. I have learned through bitter experience that if you appear to have a lot, and you generously give to those who have less, and you ask nothing in return, they could attack you and hate you. Why? This is one of those human mysteries I cannot fathom yet, but the best way to explain it with a parable from the holy book. The parable goes like this,

> There was once a very rich man who had a huge mansion with a big family and lots of servants. They ate banquets every night and lived in luxury. The very rich man was kind, loving and generous, and the ways of making money with fair, honest trade were easy and natural to him.
>
> On the streets of the village lived a very poor, thin, filthy beggar. The very rich man used to sometimes give him a couple of coins. One day, the very rich man approached the beggar and told him that there was an empty little cottage in excellent repair at the bottom of the luxury mansion's garden, and the cottage had a quarter acre of fenced land for growing crops, and it was available for the beggar to live in for free if he wanted it. The beggar was delighted and gratefully moved in.
>
> Then the very rich man went down to the cottage and ensured the beggar had everything he needed, and he told the beggar that if he wanted, he could also have all the scraps from the banquet table because sometimes there were unspoiled legs of lamb or other foods, and even if the food was spoiled, it would make excellent compost and chicken food. The beggar was delighted and grateful and accepted the offer.

All went well for several months, and then the beggar began to resent and covet the very rich man's possessions, luxury, lifestyle and ability to give so generously. He began to complain to his friends in the village how unfair it was that he lived in a tiny cottage while the rich lived in such splendour. He began to complain that he lived on scraps off the rich man's table. His hatred grew and grew until he despised the rich man. He became bitter and nasty, complaining now that he lived in a filthy little shack while … and soon he had persuaded a large portion of the population to hate the loving, generous very rich man. It is called 'bread of shame'

I have given generously before only to be hated and stolen from too, and I can't even begin to explain it, but people who have won the lottery and given generously have also discovered the existence of 'bread of shame'. Those they gave generously to did not remain grateful for long. Instead they soon became bitter, jealous and even vicious. For some reason, when you give generously, very generously to people, they cannot just accept it with grace and gratitude. It robs them of their dignity. It makes them feel 'less' and they blame you for it, or they grow an assumption that they have a right to it, or they invent reasons why it is only fair they should have it, and they convince themselves that you should have given them even more.

How to say no without feeling guilty

If you didn't have the courage to say no, then whose fault is it you've been used? Being a victim, martyr or doormat is a choice. If you are making that choice, stop it! It's bad for you and your relationships. If you don't want to give, you can and should say no!

When you need to say no without feeling guilty, remember that:

- Obedience to other people's expectations of you often means disobedience to yourself.
- Value yourself more than you value other people's expectations or opinion of you.
- Victims, martyrs and doormats are weak, unlikeable people. Don't be one.
- Hold on to your power. Do not give it away.
- You are creating your own reality. Is this the reality you want?
- The art of attraction is working for you. What sort of person are you attracting into your space and why?
- Remember the art of allowing. You are not allowing yourself to say no! Why?
- Are you being honest with yourself and with the other person? Do you really want the consequences of being dishonest just because you are afraid of being totally honest with them?
- What is worse: fear of confrontation or fear of being a doormat, recognising all the massive complications and consequences that could result?
- You *are* responsible for yourself and your happiness but not for the comfort and convenience of others.

Payments for guilt

Some people try to ease their own feelings of guilt by giving things, effort or gifts to others, or to those they feel they have hurt or wronged. If the receiver of our gifts does not know that the giving is supposed to be a pay-off or a peace offering, then how can we expect them to accept it as such? What usually happens instead is the receiver, still feeling angry, bitter or hurt, does not want anything from the one who has wronged them.

Giving to them then only makes them feel blackmailed or manipulated. We could multiply the damage we were hoping to correct. Perhaps what they really need, and all they really want, is acknowledgement or an apology. If someone throws your gift back in your face, be patient, understanding and allowing. Take it as a sign that you *really* hurt them this time, and now they have got even. Give them the gift again later. That's double quits.

Favours

We offer to do favours for people thinking that favours buy us shares. Favours buy us nothing. A favour is free help offered from the goodness of the heart. It is never a savings account or a credit card. We can tell others, before we do favours for them, that we expect the favours to buy us shares in their 'good books' or that we might call on them to do us a favour in return some time, or else we must do the favour and leave it at that. We must, however, realise that it is fair to give them a choice of what favour they do in return. What is easy for you to do, might be very hard for me to do or vice versa.

For example, you may love driving around in your car. So if you fetch my child from school one day when you are in the neighbourhood, it would be no big deal for you. If you then ask me to pick up something for you while I am in the city, and I hate driving, and I struggle to find parking space, and I get stressed in traffic, then it may be a major inconvenience for me. Perhaps I'll have to pay for parking and walk a long way. I may feel you have you demanded far too much from me, while you might see it as an equal exchange.

Likewise, if I have a good income and you are struggling financially, and I lend you £1,000 which you can't pay back, I would hurt both you and myself if I scorned your cookies that you made for me as a thank you. Being bitter against others is a silly choice. We all do the best we can, based on what we feel we are capable of. I should be delighted that you made me cookies, and tell you I don't mind waiting for the money as long as you give it back in bits (or I could forget I ever lent it to you if I want to).

A friend of mine decided to cook up some elaborate, scrumptious wraps one day, and he piled up all kinds of yummy things to fill them with. He offered my teenage son a wrap. My son looked at all the goodies and delightfully said, 'Yes, thanks, wow!' My friend made a terrible mess of the kitchen while he cooked. When they finished eating, he said to my son, 'Since I made us the scrumptious wraps, you must wash up dishes and tidy the kitchen. That's only fair.' My son looked at the terrible mess and dirty frying pans and gasped in dismay, almost choking on the last mouthful he had just swallowed. I leaped to my son's defence and explained that if my friend had explained in the first place that he would be willing to make my son a scrumptious wrap if my son would be willing to wash up and clean the kitchen afterwards, my son may well have said 'no thanks' to the wrap. My son felt he had been tricked into cleaning up for my friend. So in the end, they cleaned up together.

Ungrateful children

Too many parents use their children as a means to get praise, credit and gratitude. In the name of 'good manners' they force their children to lavish on them huge gratitude, praise and credit for all the things parents naturally do. They forget that children do not have a choice. Children cannot get food, transport, housing, lifts, birthday presents and parties from anyone but their parents. Children need to take all those things as a given, as a right, because it is very good for their self-esteem, their confidence and their sense of value. Teaching them to say 'thank you' is good and healthy, but assessing how grateful you think they are is destructive, counterproductive and can in some cases even be abusive.

When we try to force our children to be grateful, we get resentment instead. We also unconsciously teach the children that they are not worth the good things they get. We can teach them to be grateful by gentle teaching, not by demanding gratitude after we've given. Loaded giving makes them feel terrible - not grateful. It makes them feel worthless, as if they don't deserve all those good things. Children need to take their basic survival for granted, and their birthdays and other celebration gifts and treats as standard just because they are special and deserve it for no reason at all other than the fact that they are special and loved. This way the kids will know that they are valuable and worth lots and lots to their parents.

We can teach a child to be grateful through stories that explain the concept, and through helping them show gratitude to others who have been kind. We should also remember to show them gratitude when they are kind to us. We can explain in a loving and diplomatic way when we are feeling used or unappreciated. If we explain it as our feelings and not their fault, they can take it very well and learn from it. If we use accusations and guilt, we never get genuine gratitude from them but only resentment and hurt instead. We also instil in them guilt, inadequacy and low self-esteem. Some of us picked up our own deep-rooted guilt problems from our parents through this kind of thing.

When we give to our children, we are giving to *our own* children. Not to independent other people who happen to live in our home, sponging off us. The credit we get lies in the fact that we give our children good things, and our children are privileged because of us. We get social mileage out of giving our kids good things. It looks good on us. Being a good parent has its own plentiful, rich rewards.

Giving is a free act of spontaneous love

Who can put a price on love? Who can buy love? Who can give love and then demand gratitude or something in exchange? When is love ever for sale or up for bargain? Love has got to be given freely, and love can be earned in return by being genuine, loving and undemanding over time. It cannot be acquired by manipulation, extraction, expectation or force. When we give, we must give out of our love. We must never give out of our need, and we must be honest about it if we expect in return, and we must not give too generously without exchange because we might trigger 'bread of shame' (or spoil the children and make them demanding).

Giving to our friends makes us good friends, giving to our neighbours makes us good neighbours. Giving makes us good people because it feeds our love. It feels good because it is good, as long as it is noble, loving and unselfish. We should be careful to give only what and when we can really afford to give, and actually want to give. Giving when we ourselves are needy is a mistake. We deplete what little we have and leave ourselves drained or short. The lifeboat analogy says get yourself into the lifeboat first. We have to save ourselves before we can save anybody else. If we try to save people when we ourselves are drowning in the water, we go down with the people we mean to save - and they blame us.

There is one kind of giving that immediately causes you to receive just by giving, and that is love. But the receiving comes from the process of feeling love within ourselves and not necessarily from the other. When we give love, in the act of giving it, we feel full of love in our hearts. We feel the love inside ourselves as we are giving it and therefore we are giving ourselves love simultaneously. We can't not. It is not possible to give love without feeling it and enjoying it inside ourselves as we give it. It is an immediately self-rewarding thing in its self. It is a process of self-enrichment as well as a blessing for mankind. The more we give it, the more it grows in us, and therefore the more we have of it. Being a loving person is a lovely feeling. Being in love is one of the greatest feelings on earth.

Enjoy giving. It affords you an abundance mentality. There is no such thing as an ungrateful person, only a disappointed giver. And disappointment is a choice.

I'm counting the fear
Of holding you dear
And wondering what is the price
I'm getting too old
To cope with the cold
I don't want you just to be nice

I have all this love
Yet somewhere above
Bigger than that I'm afraid
I see you withhold
I feel you grow cold
I see your attention has strayed

You're so many things
And all of them brings
Yet more dimensions of you
I look and I stare
Cause somewhere in there
Is mystery and magic so new

Will you be mine
Soon or in time
Perhaps we will never quite gel
What do you feel
And what is real
If only my wisdom could tell

Oh to carefree hold on
And fly like a swan
And let my love blossom and grow
Would be such bliss
But what if I miss
My grief would be awful I know

By Terri Ann Laws

Conflict Management

There are many different styles or ways people have of dealing with conflict. Here is a humorous way of looking at the different conflict styles. Do you recognize any of these styles in the people you know? Can you pick out your own style?

D. Niyal: Buries his head in the sand and says, 'What conflict? There's no conflict.'

F. Ducker: Disappears. He says, 'I'm out of here.' 'I'm not getting involved.'

S. Willing: Is willing to do just about anything to keep the peace, saying, 'I hate trouble. I'll make it better. I'll do anything for peace.'

Jo Jolly: Bursts out laughing. He thinks making light of it, seeing it as funny or making it entertaining will somehow dilute the problem.

X. Plainaway: Rationalizes. He says, 'It's all very simple really …' 'Well obviously people could feel upset when …' 'It's probably quite understandable that …' He launches into explanations, reasons and logic.

B. Bull: Overpowers. He assumes a position of absolute authority and dares anyone to question or contradict him. He appears powerful or enormous or dangerous or threatening, so no one will dare confront him.

I. Great: Is self-righteous. He is dogmatic, judgemental and absolutely sure that he is right and you are wrong. He launches into the 'I-me-I-me' monologue telling you what he wants, thinks, needs, feels, expects and what you should, ought, must do etc…

O. Dunno: Stares blankly with wide eyes. You never know what he is feeling. He probably doesn't know half the time either. He just thinks and thinks and thinks and thinks

B. Saime: Conforms, adapts, wants to be the same as everyone else. He just goes along and agrees. He doesn't express his own beliefs or feelings. He says you're absolutely right and he tries to convince himself you are right. He is compelled to have the consensual opinion as his own.

A. Loof: Is aloof. He thinks that confrontation is way beneath him. He is far too superior to engage in such things. He looks down on people who confront.

D. Zarster: Looks at you with bewildered, sad eyes and a hurt, shocked look. The message is, 'Oh no! There isn't a problem is there?' 'You're not going to be upset with me now are you?' Some D. Zarsters actually do burst into tears. They rely on your pity to avoid conflict. They throw their helplessness or hurt at you to stop you from confronting them.

Will Givantake: Is happy to compromise. He is happy to give a little if you are too. He looks for a fair, agreeable exchange. He's into bargaining. He says, 'I'll meet you halfway'

Patient N Strong: Values relationships. He wants both you and himself to be very happy with the arrangement with no resentment downstream. He is patient and willing to confront and stay in the negotiation process for as long as it takes. He has full consideration for you and full courage to confront. He wants to find an even better way than compromise. He is happy to deal with conflict. He doesn't want to compromise and he doesn't want you to have to compromise either. He has a lot of patience and is willing to brainstorm and discuss and look further a-field in an attempt to make sure everyone gets the best arrangement.

All these ways of dealing with conflict are actually ways of avoiding conflict ... except the Patient N Strong way.

The most successful way to manage conflict is the way Patient N Strong handles it. Don't avoid the conflict like all the others do; embrace it. Keep talking, looking for more possible solutions, getting more feelings, truth and honesty out, discussing possibilities, being willing to really listen without interrupting. Be brave enough to be honest about what you really want, and strong enough to look for solutions and not villains. Be determined to find a solution that everyone is happy with - even if it takes a long time.

Understanding conflict

First let's look at relationships and issues. The conflict styles we choose are dependent mostly on two variables. firstly, how important the issue is, and secondly how important the relationship is.

When we have taken a faulty item back to a shop, the relationship we have with the salesman is of minor importance compared to the issue. We may resort to B. Bull if the salesman is being difficult. When an angry boss is accusing us, we may choose X. Plainaway, because the relationship and the issue are both important. When a loved one has burst into tears and becomes very upset as a result of the conflict, we may abandon the issue in favour of the relationship and become S. Willing.

When the relationship is more important than the issue, we need to remember to behave very differently than we might do when the issue is more important than the relationship. It is vital for us to get our priorities straight when engaging in conflict to make sure we do not hurt special people by wanting to be right. Such an action has far reaching implications and can lead to far more and far worse conflict in the long run. This type of short-sightedness is what causes most 'teenage rebellion' and ongoing domestic fighting. (There is no such thing as teenage rebellion by the way, as you will discover, if you haven't already.)

Courage and consideration

Another way of looking at it is the balance between courage and consideration. If we are high on courage but low on consideration, we may push to get our own way and be willing to fight with people. We could choose B. Bull or A. Loof and not care if the other person is suffering. If we are

159

high on consideration but low on courage, we may be afraid of offending or afraid of consequences, and so choose the D. Zarster, D. Niyal or F. Ducker option.

We need to acquire an equal balance of courage and consideration so that we have enough courage to confront and deal with the issue, yet have enough consideration for the other to make sure that they are not hurt, confused or angered in the process.

If we are high on courage only, we may be assertive and find ourselves competing or controlling. If we are high on consideration only, we may be afraid and uneasy, and find ourselves accepting, accommodating or giving in resentfully and losing all the time.

If we are high on both courage and consideration, we may be cooperative and find ourselves collaborating, compromising and finding effective solutions.

If we are low on both courage and consideration, we may be totally avoiding doing much about anything or anyone and avoid conflict completely, the O. Dunno style, and perhaps A. Loof.

Trust
We first need to recognise, understand and deal with our own fears, inner feelings and inner conflict before we are able to understand and empathise with another's. When the trust level is high, it's easier to be open. When the trust level is low, we may find people avoiding, manipulating, exaggerating or sharing only part of the facts and feelings. In order to get to the bottom of a conflict situation and fix it so that it does not come up again, we need to communicate on a deeper level. The depth of

communication is dependent on the level of trust in the relationship.

If you go for win/lose, this means that someone has won and someone has lost. This damages the relationship. If one wins, the other is left feeling bad (angry, resentful, cheated, hurt, betrayed, rebellious, embarrassed, whatever.). Things will come up again and again in later issues. In most relationships, people are more important than issues. Issues come and go daily, but relationships last much longer. A good general rule of thumb is never sacrifice people for issues because if you do, future issues will be far more serious, difficult or frequent. The only exception is when the issue is very important to you and you couldn't give a hoot about the person and you have no reason to ever see or deal with that person again, and you have a very good reason for winning on the issue.

Conflict is normal, healthy and growth inspiring. It should be seen as an opportunity to know others and our selves better. Conflict can never be avoided without adverse consequences. When we try to avoid conflict, all we really do is push it underground where it festers and grows and causes all kinds of other problems.

Building better relationships in the face of conflict

Valuing the people and the relationship is the art of effective conflict management. People are more important than things. The issue at hand is a tiny matter compared to the people involved. It doesn't matter how enormous or important you think the issue is, it is never and can never be as important as the people involved and your relationship with them. If you never lose sight of this fact, managing conflict becomes a lot easier.

Things to consider before confronting

How upset am I? If I feel I am too worked up emotionally, I can ask for time out for five minutes to cool down and gather my thoughts and feelings.

How upset are they? If they are too worked up emotionally, give them space and time to cool off, calm down and gather their thoughts and feelings. Remember the art of allowing. If they are shouting and accusing and going off on one, just detach and allow it, just stare at them without speaking or showing any emotion at all. Once they have vented, they will calm down. Then begin with the Patient N Strong method of conflict management.

How important is this to me? to them? to others? Evaluating who and what is at stake helps to understand why some people may be blowing things way out of proportion. I may feel the matter is trivial while others may feel that it is a vital, serious matter of great importance. It is a mistake to invalidate others by saying something like, 'Pull yourself together' 'It is no big deal' assuming that our assessment of the situation is the only true reality. People can feel some very strong emotions if they think their values, rules or principles are being violated. Just because you think it is trivial does not mean the other should think so too. If they think it is trivial and you think it is very important, then it is important for you to calmly point this fact out to them. Tell them you appreciate that they see it as trivial, and that's OK, but to you it is not trivial at all, but vitally important.

What could be the long-term results or consequences if it goes wrong? This is a very important assessment and should not be made lightly. Winning the battle now could mean losing the war later. Demanding that you get the respect you think you deserve from your teenager now, could result in a hostile, cold war for months or even years. Disciplining a subordinate now could kill any chance of long-term loyalty and trust they may have had in you. Punishing the child when the child feels it is unfair could damage the child and your relationship with him/her. Consider the consequences to the dynamics of the relationship. Look for a more ecological solution.

What do I actually hope to achieve eventually? Keep your desired outcome in mind. Picture what you do want, not only what you don't want. Head for the ideal outcome and don't lose sight of it in the heat of the moment. Clarify all your expectations and allow others to do the same. Discuss the ideal situation between you first if possible, and then work on the area of conflict. First, find at least one area of agreement. With the end in mind it is so much easier to reach a win/win solution that everyone is happy with. Watch out for ego and foolish pride! These are dangerous stumbling blocks to effective conflict management. A little humility, compassion, patience and understanding along with the courage to confront, can push you streets ahead in achieving what you ultimately want to achieve through the conflict.

Never see conflict as a bad thing. Since it cannot be avoided, there is no point in viewing it this way. See it as necessary, normal and unavoidable. It is an excellent opportunity to know others and yourself better. Consider the alternatives. Pretending that everything is fine? Forcing

163

everything to be fine? Feeling miserable and desperate because everything is not fine? Being afraid to admit that things aren't fine?

Let's not confuse conflict with fighting. Fighting is when the conflict has gone out of control and two individuals have resorted to attacking each other - verbally or physically. Both wanting to be the only one who is right, or to bring each other down, punishing each other or getting even. Fighting is often the result of unmanaged conflict that has gone wrong lots of times in the past. Or a result of repeatedly avoiding conflict over time until someone snaps. Fighting is also what control freaks and bullies do to avoid conflict.

We can assume that conflict is fighting because it so often ends up that way - but it doesn't have to. We can learn the skills necessary to avoid things going wrong. We are all multifaceted, diverse and complex human beings. It is totally unreasonable to hope for, or strive for, a life free of conflict. Where there is no conflict, it's a sign that nobody cares anymore. They have sunken into apathy, withdrawal and disinterest. If conflict is avoided, you can be sure that somebody is getting hurt, angry or disappointed. Somebody is burying a whole lot of feelings, or being a victim or a martyr or a doormat. It is not possible for all of us to always agree on everything indefinitely. That's just not the nature of human beings.

When we engage in healthy, constructive conflict, we build strong, honest, free and lasting relationships, because we build trust, truth and integrity into our relationships. We get a hearing, we voice our opinions, we listen to others and we become involved with each other.

164

It's only when we don't know where we stand and when we don't know how others feel that we get insecure - which leads to us being arbitrary and defensive in an attempt to protect ourselves. Once both parties know where they stand and how the other feels, negotiations can run smoothly and constructively.

If you want your relationships to be pleasant and to last - business, personal or domestic, then confront every issue immediately, or as soon as it is safe and feasible to do so. Confront with honesty, truth, consideration and courage. Allow the conflict, and manage it like Patient N Strong. Nobody must win at anybody else's expense. Everybody must be validated and respected. All cards must go down on the table. Then everybody knows what everyone else wants and thinks, and there are no squashed feelings or hidden agendas lurking somewhere to ruin the relationship downstream. Powerful bonds of trust and permanence are built this way and will stand the test of time, any test of any time.

Basic points to remember
- It is impossible to live in peace and harmony constantly with other humans without ever having any conflict.
- We are all very different, and sooner or later, we will always find an area where we disagree.
- The right thing is to discuss it. The wrong thing is to avoid discussing it.
- Disagreement is a fact of life, not a problem of life.
- Pretending that everything is all right does not keep the peace. It causes resentment, which leads to far more conflict later.

- You cannot be inwardly upset and outwardly happy for very long.
- There is something about everyone that annoys you, even your true love, even your children, even your favourite best friends. They all have at least one little thing that annoys you or you don't like. This is normal, not bad. There is something about you that they don't like too.
- Pretending causes inner conflict. Inner conflict causes anger, hurt, frustration, stress, irritation and revenge. It is like walking with a stone in your shoe.
- Inner conflict always leads to outer conflict - sooner or later. If you are afraid to fight with the person who has 'made you tense or upset', you will fight with someone else to relieve the pressure, or you could get physically ill.
- We are not guilty of the things others find wrong with us. If I am irritated by a blunt approach, and to me your approach seems blunt, it does not mean you are guilty of something. It only means I am irritated by your approach, which to me seems blunt. It's my interpretation and presses my personal buttons, therefore it's my responsibility and not yours.
- I cannot blame you, but I must tell you - in the kindest way I can. It is my irritation, not your fault. If I don't tell you, then I will continue to feel irritated. If I do tell you, I can stop feeling that way.
- We hurt our ourselves and our relationships with other people much more by using conflict avoidance tactics than we do by honestly conflicting with them. But we don't have to choose between silence and war!
- We can learn to be honest and considerate.

166

- It takes a lot of courage at first to change, but with practice it very quickly becomes easy, and it pays off in so many beneficial ways.

- Complaining to someone else instead of the person you are feeling conflict towards, causes a lot of trouble. It spreads negativity. It can create a war zone. It can put everyone into different camps, and it can earn you many more enemies than friends. The worst-case scenario if you always try to get people in your corner is that people might no longer trust you - especially those people you have been 'gossiping' too! When you run into conflict with them, they know all too well that you look for people in your corner. They know you try to get a whole lot of people on your side. It's possible that before long almost everyone will dislike you and hardly anyone will trust you. Be careful not to let this happen to you, and if you know of someone who does this, you'll be doing them a great favour if you point it out to them.

- If you want to be trusted, be trustworthy. If you want honesty from others, be honest yourself. If you want to know where you stand with people, tell them where they stand with you. If you want people to level with you, level with them. If you want people to like you, like them first. If you want to be loved, become lovable. If you want to be respected, become worthy of respect and treat others with respect.

May your conflict and confrontations be smooth and constructive in future and may they lead to great growth, understanding and bonds of trust.

Can you be gentle no matter what?
Can you be loving with all that you've got?
Can you be tolerant, allowing and free?
Can you accept things just like you see?

Can you replenish so you have enough?
And be responsible for your own stuff?
Can you get strength from your self inside?
Can you contain your own hurt, your own pride?

Can you survive life's crushing blows?
And notice the feedback it teaches and shows?
Can you find comfort and nurture yourself?
And pick yourself up, put you back on the shelf?

Can you look outward and see other's pain?
And not weigh it up against what you might gain?
Can you have the courage to stand up and speak?
And yet considerate enough to be meek?

Is your mind open, is your heart clean?
What will you do when you want to be mean?
How will you handle your anger or hurt?
Can you sling flowers instead of dirt?

by Terri Ann Laws

Hot Emotional Buttons!

How do you feel when someone pushes your buttons?

Whose fault is it when someone makes you angry, hurt, jealous, insecure or embarrassed?   Is it your fault if someone else suddenly and unexpectedly gets that way as a result of something you did or said?

So it's their fault if you get upset with them, and it's their fault if they get upset with you??? It sounds ridiculous, but this is what automatically happens all the time. We know our reasons and intentions, and we expect others to know them too. If not, we merely explain our good intentions and then we think that will make everything all right. We expect that if they push our buttons, we only need explain to them that it is a button for us, and they will stop it.

What we are actually expecting is that they change their behaviour for our convenience (because we explained about our button), but we don't have to change our behaviour for their convenience (because we explained about our intentions). When we look at this logically and fairly, we realise how unbalanced and one-sided it is.

Our buttons are our own responsibility. If someone pushes our buttons, it's our fault for having the button in the first place. Our buttons are our weaknesses. They are a result of our earlier programming. As long as we have buttons, we are vulnerable and at the mercy of others who can push them by default or design. Other people can take control over how we feel. If someone you spend time with knows a certain word makes you angry, then all she needs to do to ruin your day is say that word at you. Essentially that means she has complete control over you whenever she wants it, and can make you as miserable as she wants to any time she likes. When those you spend time with know what your buttons are, they can manipulate you to their convenience. They have the power to decide whether or not you'll be happy today!

Oh, how powerful the mighty button is, and few people really realise how vulnerable they make themselves by reacting to their own buttons. Here is a very scary thought for you to contemplate: if your partner knows what makes you insecure, he can prevent you from leaving him by making you insecure every time you try. If your boss knows what makes you afraid, she can use that to control you too. If your kids know what makes you feel guilty, they can use that well to their advantage. You are the victim of anyone once they know what your buttons are and then they have the power to make it so you cannot enjoy life without their permission. You are a puppet in their hands *only if* you have not taken responsibility for your own buttons. The good news is that you can - and certainly should - disconnect all of your hot emotional buttons.

Our buttons are only our understanding of what is meant or implied by certain words or deeds. If we change our understanding (or interpretation) of what those words or deeds suggest or imply, we dis-empower the button. Our beliefs, values and perceptions have our buttons embedded in them. We need to examine the way we interpret things, because deep within our automatic assumptions about the way things really are (or ought to be) lurk the beliefs that caused our buttons.

For example, if your parents always said to you when you were small, 'You sneaky little cheat!' with a big smile and a hug every time you did some clever, responsible thing all on your own without asking for help, and without even bragging about it afterwards, you would then have no problem as an adult if someone accused you of being a sneaky little cheat. You would probably beam and gloat and make some smart comment like, 'Some of us are wide awake!' There would be absolutely no pain or anger attached to that insult because to you it would imply a compliment. You wouldn't feel hurt, you'd feel powerful, even when you know they meant to offend you. Your childhood programming would override the facts in the moment and your neurology would be conditioned deep within you to feel complimented in response to being called sneaky or called a cheat.

Let's pretend for a moment that I had parents who accused me of being selfish, and consequently I had devoted my entire life to proving them wrong. Showing the world how utterly unselfish I am would be of vital importance to me. It could even become an obsession. I could work my fingers to the bone, give constantly without accepting reward, become a doormat, put everyone first, do everything for anyone, desperate to hear a few words just one more time, and the words would be: 'She is so unselfish, so giving, so sharing, so caring ….' Just imagine what fun an abusive person could have with me. Also, I could get angry to the point of exploding if someone kept accusing me of being selfish. Every time I thought someone doubted my unselfishness, I'd prove categorically, without a shadow of doubt that I am completely unselfish in every way, no matter how much trouble I needed to put myself through. Imagine what a powerful, blinding button that could be? Imagine how anyone could manipulate me?

I could unknowingly sacrifice my whole life to proving an obvious fact to people, many of whom would take advantage of the situation. What power people would hold over me! They could get me to be grateful to be allowed to do anything! They could make me blissfully happy or utterly miserable by using just one silly little accusation that does not have to have a shred of truth in it.

What buttons do you have? How have people pulled your strings? What accusation gets you to jump up and do stuff? Are there things you're still trying to prove to people who have either long gone or don't deserve your great sacrifices and efforts?

Steps towards disempowering our buttons
In order to disconnect all your buttons, the first thing to realize or remember is that all words and actions have absolutely no meaning other than the meaning given by the individual. We interpret words and actions the way we do

because we are 'seeing' (interpreting) through the eyes of our own unique understanding and all its implications for us in our own unique way based on the experiences we've had, and the sense we've made of those experiences. A hundred different people will have a hundred different reactions to the one same word or phrase. No reaction to any button is objectively out there in the world. All reactions to any button are inside the neurology of the person who experiences it , and sometimes do not even relate to objective shared reality.

Through the wonderful human capacity of selective memory we can single out all the great, fun memories from when we were small (even if they were few) and talk for hours about them. Or we can single out all the painful memories (and feel all those feelings again) and talk for hours about them. No one runs our minds but ourselves. Our minds run our emotions. We can examine our thoughts. We can choose which memories to run and we can change our neurological response to any memory and watch our thoughts and memories with curious fascination and laugh at ourselves. We can do this if we choose to.

We can also look at terrible experiences from the past, review them, and this time sympathize with the perpetrator. We can rearrange our memories, we can re- interpret our experiences. We can change the meaning we attach to anything at all. This is the most fantastic thing about the human mind. We can do incredible things with it. We can control our own thinking, our entire perception of what reality is and this is why we can free ourselves of our buttons. This is how we get rid of our buttons.

Buttons Busting

There are four steps to Button Busting. Find the button (or admit to having it). Find the meaning you have. Find the expectation you have. The last step is to change your meaning and change your expectation. Then you won't have the button anymore.

Select a button you want to disconnect. Think about the meaning you give to it. For example, Button: 'My daughter rolls her eyes at me and it makes me raging mad.' Meaning: 'She has no respect for me.'

Remember, the meaning is *your* meaning and not *the* meaning, because someone else might give a different meaning. For example, someone else might decide it means that they approached her wrong, or that she is manipulative, or she is feeling frustrated, or the relationship wants building or something else.

Having got the button, having discovered the meaning you're giving it, now think about what you expected to happen instead. For example, 'I expected to her to say, "Yes Mum." Or perhaps you expected her to do something or smile, or explain politely why she didn't want to or whatever. Once you've realized what you were expecting or what you expect, you can question yourself and ask yourself why you expect that. Is it OK to expect that? Would it be more useful to expect something else instead?

Teenagers behave like teenagers. When you expect them to behave as something else, you are bound to suffer some button triggering. The meaning is not that they are bad or you are bad, the meaning is because they have too many hormones, and they need to exert their independence and discover new boundaries as they change from child to adult. If you expect them to behave as teenagers behave, you'll not have an emotional response anymore, you'll be able to choose an intelligent response.

If you find and identify all your buttons, you give yourself tremendous freedom and reclaim all your power. Take full responsibility for them. Find out how they got there, where they originated, your earliest memory of feeling that way in response to that thing or word. Change your interpretations. Be grateful when someone presses one of your buttons because that's how you know it's there, that's how you know what to work on, that's how you know where you are still vulnerable and what area needs more attention. Broaden the gap between the stimulus you receive and your response to it, and then choose an appropriate response. This is the ultimate mental combat. Mental victory in this area will be a vital victory in your control over your own life, circumstances and happiness.

I wish you strength, hope, staying power and victory over all your buttons.

The Shortage Mentality

The shortage mentality is a belief that there is a limited amount of everything. There are only so many top positions, only so many people who can become famous or millionaires, only so much money, only so many great achievements to be made or things to be conquered. One who has this belief suffers a sad feeling of loss whenever someone they know, especially someone close to them, gets windfall luck or a big promotion or fame or recognition and although they genuinely congratulate the person, deep inside they feel a strange sense of loss because that other person got there first. The other person's success in some odd way almost feels like their failure.

The reason they feel this way is because they imagine that since the other person got it that means it's taken and no longer available, or they might imagine it's going to be so much harder now to match up or achieve or compete. Their value and self- worth seems threatened. So even though they are thrilled for their friends or loved ones, somewhere deep inside they feel deprived, uncomfortable, and less. They feel there is less left, or since someone got there first, there is less chance and opportunity. They feel robbed of the prize, the credit, the glory, the luck.

This is the shortage mentality and it is way out of touch with reality. If you have a shortage mentality, you will see lack in many other areas of your life too. It can create a sense of urgency, of competition, of fear or insecurity. If there really was a limited amount of opportunities and resources, then this feeling would make sense and be valid, but there is absolutely no scarcity of any sort in the world at

176

all. Whenever anything begins to run out, opportunity seekers, creative people and great thinkers very quickly find alternatives and rush to make money out of it or to get recognition for discovering it. Lack or shortage always creates huge growth and expansion, which in turn creates even more opportunities.

The shortage mentality can have you seeing lack or shortage everywhere:

- Afraid to give, feeling you have to hold on to what you've got.
- Afraid of losing anything because you might never get it again.
- Not enough say at work - your opinion isn't taken seriously enough.
- Not enough jobs out there, so it's best to hold on to this terrible one.
- Not enough financial worth to persuade the bank to give you an overdraft.
- Not enough talent or ability or opportunity to do the things you dream of.
- Lack and 'not enough' in your children, they do not get high enough achievements, they do not give enough appreciation, do not have enough friends...
- Your partner lacks many traits or qualities
- You don't get enough attention, respect, love...
- You can't afford this and you can't afford that.
- There are too many businesses and not enough customers.
- The economy is bad, there is a shortage of money, a shortage of resources.

- There is no point in starting my own business because there is not enough something or other. It would definitely fail.
- Running out of time, getting too old, it's too late.

Add your favourite fear of lack here......

The shortage mentality causes us to see want, lack and scarcity wherever we look. 'Less than' is a frame of mind. It has no basis in fact. Most millionaires are only millionaires in theory, because the more they turn over, the more they spend on growing and expanding, relying on turnover and potential rather than accumulated savings. They work on projected figures not accumulated capital. Money sitting in the bank is dead money - the interest does not even keep up with the inflation rate. Money in circulation grows at a very much faster rate, in fact it can double and double again in a matter of months. Being a millionaire or billionaire doesn't mean you have money in the bank, it means you have learned how to get money to flow in the world. It is a skill in your head and a belief in your heart and it has nothing to do with your bank balance.

For example, a property investor who owns twenty houses which she rents out is in fact in massive, massive debt, but she doesn't see it that way. She has mortgages on each property, so one way of looking at it is that she owes the bank several million. The other way of looking at it is to realise that each property brings in rent higher than the mortgage repayments, and so she gets a bit off the top from each property. Her properties are worth whatever the market says they are worth, and she sees that as her wealth, not the total amount of all her mortgages.

The shortage mentality is based on fear. Fear of losing, fear of getting left behind, fear of going without, fear of missing something. This fear is debilitating. It causes stress, insomnia, depression, panic, stinginess and all kinds of things. It creates a feeling of vulnerability and insecurity. It causes us to deny ourselves so many things, thinking we can't afford it, thinking we can't have it or don't deserve it. It causes us to stay in a bad situation far too long, to hang on to a job that is under-paying or overworking us, or to spend twenty years wishing for something, never getting to the point where we feel we deserve it or can afford it. Always seeing some or other lack as the reason why we can't have, do or be what we want.

The mentality of plenty

This is recognizing that there are vast resources out there to be collected or created. There are millions of possibilities, millions of opportunities, millions of ideas, millions of customers. There is an endless supply of everything. There is no limit to the amount of No.1 positions since there are millions of areas to be the No.1 in, and more areas can be created. Even the No.1 in our own chosen area cannot stay there forever. We can compete in a positive, exciting way, or we can create a new unique stage. We can do whatever we like. We can let others win without losing a thing.

There is always space for more books on the shelf no matter how many have already been written. There are always fans for every new artist. There is always a way wherever there is a will. There is always space for more stars, more heroes, more achievers and more new products. There is always time to do it. No one and nothing is running out.

The mentality of plenty sets us free. It helps us set others free in our hearts as well. It helps us feel thrilled inside as well as outside when others achieve or get lucky. We can look at them and say, 'Gosh if they did it, so can I.' We can ask them to show us how they did it. It gives us courage to break free and make something happen. It gives us a vision to dream up new things to create. It widens our horizons and makes us bigger as people. It gives us power and hope and enthusiasm.

The mentality of shortage is a lie. The mentality of plenty is the truth. It's the people with the mentality of plenty that bring out new things, and invent stuff and open up businesses. They are the ones who make things happen and create jobs. They see plenty and so they go out and get some. If we see lack, we hang on jealously to what little we've got, afraid of parting with a penny or a thing. We close ourselves in to a limited narrow world. We have to believe in plenty before we can be free to grow financially. We have to be convinced that there is plenty more where that came from. We have to believe in plenty to let go of jealousy.

Lack, want and shortage are only states of mind. When there really is a lack of something, the whole world knows about it, and that only sparks enterprising people into creating an alternative. A lack of employment means you can pick and choose your staff. A lack of cash causes dozens of moneylenders to open up business. A shortage of rice makes the wheat farmers rich. A real shortage anywhere actually means great opportunities of plenty somewhere else.

The mentality of plenty will help you see so much further and wider. It will disintegrate all your paradigms of lack, 'not enough', or want, including your domestic, financial and personal ones. It will combat any feelings of jealousy you may have experienced as a result of the success of others. You don't have to be jealous of anyone for any reason. Look at your life. What do you think you lack? In how many places do you see 'not enough'? Does this tell you something? Change your mind and believe there is plenty and you'll begin to see plenty where you used to see shortage. You'll see whatever it is you look for. Look for lack and you'll find it, look for plenty and you'll find it, because it is only a state of mind and you can change your mind. Spread your wings! The world is huge! Your dreams are waiting for you with outstretched arms and a huge welcoming grin.

Doing it Badly

Anything worth doing, is worth doing badly. If you don't keep learning new things, you may never discover your full potential. You may well be clipping the wings that could take you to greatness. Who knows? You could be robbing yourself of a spectacular career in an entirely different field.

If you were not willing to do a thing badly, you would never attempt anything you could not already do well. You couldn't learn anything new, and as time marched on and others were learning new things, your problem would grow. In order to do anything well one needs to practise, and practice starts with the first attempt. There are very few people out there who can get something right first try, and if they do, they usually find that beginners' luck follows with a harsh reality slap when they try to repeat the first amazing performance. All things have to be learned step-by-step and practised until mastery is achieved. We limit ourselves terribly if we deny ourselves the chance to practise after making our first 'not good enough' attempt.

When children start school and learn to read and write, they are not given the choice to say, 'I'm useless at this! I have no talent! It's not for me.' It may be true they have no talent for either reading or writing. When this is the case, it takes them a few months longer than the others. Those that eventually read and/or write very well are not the ones with talent who originally learned easily, it's the ones who had to struggle to get it right - and became determined because of that. They had to learn, or they wanted to be good at it and applied themselves with practice. Those without natural talent make more distinctions and practise more and usually end up being much better at it, and more reliably better at it, because they are not depending on divine inspiration but are depending on finely tuned training.

Perfectionism is a fault that prevents us from doing so many things. Our expectation should be to slowly improve, not to be perfect. Nothing is ever perfect. Expecting to be perfect sets us up for disappointment. Perfection is in the eye of the beholder anyway. How can you compare Rembrandt with Picasso? What is perfect? Whose idea of perfect are we trying to live up to anyway? Having a hero or role model to follow makes practising more fun because we can track our progress against a standard we've chosen.

Being afraid of doing badly can be a self-fulfilling prophecy. You may do worse than you might have done just because you are so tense, afraid and convinced you can't. Expecting to do badly at first, removes a lot of pressure. It also makes trying new things a lot of fun - you can laugh at your first attempt knowing full well that it's going to be awful. It can't be anything but awful, unless you have beginner's luck. In that case, your second attempt will probably be awful. Live with it. It is a fact of life for everyone. Give yourself full permission to do badly at first. You'll always be trying new things if you're willing to do badly. Trying new things means you'll keep learning and growing and expanding your abilities, whether or not you actually master anything. You'll either master a few things or you'll become a jack- of-all-trades, but you'll be much better at everything if you are willing to try a lot of things and willing to do very, very badly at first.

We could use 'doing it badly' as a challenge. It's amazing how resourceful we can become when we put our minds to learning something. We start thinking up all sorts of ways to help ourselves learn quicker or easier. We practise our initiative. We also train ourselves in the fields of courage and patience, and that is invaluably useful in a lot of other contexts, other areas of our lives, as well.

Steps to doing more things
- Harness your fear and take risks.
- Swallow your pride and admit you're human.
- Subdue your ego and allow others to be better than you.
- Compliment others by asking them for help (or patience).
- Don't be hard on yourself or critical of yourself.
- Allow yourself as much time as you need to learn.
- Break the task into small, easy steps to learn one at a time.
- Believe in yourself and know that eventually you will get it right.

- Think of how great you will feel when you do get it right.
- Give yourself full permission to do badly many times while you're learning.
- Take yourself off the hook by saying 'I'm awful at this' before you start, or by saying 'I learn slowly' to encourage others to have patience with you. Don't actually believe what you say, just say it to comfort yourself and let yourself off the hook. What you need to believe is that you will eventually get it right and get very good at it too.

A quote I once saw was: 'If no two people are exactly alike, then each of us must be unique. If something is unique, it is the only existing sample of itself. It must therefore be perfect.' So, if you want to be perfect be exactly as you are. Your first attempts will be your own original, unique perfect first attempts.

You might be capable of much more than you realize. You'll never know unless you try - a lot more times than once. Listen to your heart (desire) not your head (fear and logic). If you have the desire to do something you probably have the potential to be good at it. If you have a very strong desire, you probably have a lot of potential to be very good at it. Besides, the more desire you have the more effort you are likely to put in. The more effort you put in, the sooner it will become easy. Good luck and enjoy your new ventures with all your heart!

Emotional Stability

In order to become emotionally stable, we need to allow our emotions to mature. There are four types of maturity; Physical, mental, spiritual and emotional.

Physical maturity happens to us whether we want it to or not. We grow up into adults.

Mental maturity can be stifled or neglected, but we reach a certain degree of it anyway.

Spiritual maturity is a choice. Some people are very spiritual, some are not interested.

Emotional maturity escapes us unless we have pondered a little on the above two. Our level of emotional stability will have a serious effect on the quality of our lives. In recent years it has become apparent that EQ (Emotional Intelligence) is far more important than IQ, even in academic fields.

Physical maturity is the only one of the four that has definite boundaries. We can clearly see the difference between a child and an adult. Since physical maturity takes care of itself, is constant, obvious and needs no help, we will ignore it for now and concentrate on the other three.

The other three have no boundaries. We can be as backwards or as advanced as you can imagine and not even know it. We need our mental capacity to evaluate how mature we are, and/or want to become. We use our spiritual capacity to find meaning, connection, religion, philosophy and a sense of belonging or purpose in life. We use our emotional capacity to feel, to love, hate, to laugh and to respond to the heart of others and to situations in life.

If I were mentally immature, I would display one or several, or perhaps even all, of the following:

- I would not want to or not be able to come to conclusions or make decisions without some help, advice or input from someone else.
- I would not want to think, decide or choose for myself unless I had some standard or external check to evaluate against.
- I would easily be confused, or fail to understand.
- I would be afraid of doing or trying new things completely on my own in case there were things I hadn't thought to consider.
- I would not be able to evaluate the intellectual input of others and come up with my own original thinking in response to it, or form my own logical argument against it.
- I would need someone to help me think through stuff or to help me to make decisions.

- I would have 'one right way' of making decisions and be unwilling or unable to discuss and contemplate other ways of thinking or deciding.
- I would not enjoy intellectual, philosophical or analytical discussions.
- I wouldn't be able to think on my feet and I'd not want to go out into the world without preparing the steps or the route or the way I should take first.

I might not know if I was mentally immature. It is not always evident to the person themselves that they are this way. It requires a thinking mind to make distinctions of depth of mental acuity and aptitude. If you've not developed your mind to make those distinctions, then you wouldn't know if you lacked mental acuity or mental maturity. We only use about 5% of our mental faculties anyway so no one has the excuse of being 'dumb' and everyone can learn to use much more of their minds.

If I were spiritually immature, I would display one or several, or perhaps even all, of the following:

- I would have little or no awe or reverence for nature, the cosmos or the beauty in art or poetry or music.
- I would have no deep thought or feeling contemplations on things like religion, philosophy, God, the destiny of mankind or anything else that is spiritual.
- I might know that I am spiritually immature, but I probably would not care.
- I would have no religion, no philosophy and I wouldn't give a thought to concepts like 'What are we on planet earth for?' or 'What is the point of all this?' or 'Where do we go when we die?'

If I were emotionally immature, I would display one or several, or perhaps even all, of the following:

- I would react to the world and to other people in terms of what it or they are doing (or have done) to me or for me.
- I would have reasons why every bad thing that ever happened to me was something or someone else's fault.
- I would often suffer from emotional outbursts, external or internal.
- I would believe that circumstances and/or other people caused my emotional outbursts.
- I would have strong reactive feelings that often blindly drive my actions and words.
- I would have very little control over how I feel. My emotions would control me rather than me controlling them.

I would definitely not know that I was emotionally immature, and if I did know, I would deny it vehemently and react badly to being accused of it.

Since there is no ceiling, no exact measurement, no one can ever become completely mature. There are vast differences in levels of maturity between ordinary, normal citizens and they all manage to live their lives anyway. Mental maturity is a choice and has little bearing on how much you enjoy life. Simple, uneducated, un-stimulated people can enjoy life just as much as well educated, well read, intellectual or highly advanced people can. In fact those people who are very simple and very mentally immature are often delightfully ignorant, happy and uncomplicated and they maintain a simple, uncomplicated existence. They don't ask for much, they don't achieve much and they don't do much and they stay faithful in one simple job for life. This is not the life for everyone, but it works for simple types, and there's no point in bothering them, and there is nothing wrong with that.

To increase mental maturity one has to go in search of knowledge, mental challenges, stretching experiences, opportunities outside of one's comfort zone and, basically, put the brain to work. Reading non-fiction books and getting into discussions with stimulating people is a good way to increase mental skills.

Spiritual maturity is also a choice. Spirituality adds a very rich quality to life and can give many things more meaning. Choosing it would lead to more inner peace, states of inner bliss, feelings of connection and belonging, and increased intuition and good luck. This has the potential to lead to improved emotional maturity too. To increase spiritual maturity it's necessary to spend time doing things such as being silent, contemplating, meditating, doing prana or yogic breathing, observing nature (staring at sunsets or endlessly rolling waves on the sea shore, or watching ants or any other things), worshiping, praying, feeling reverend and acquiring an appreciation for all things of beauty on earth and beyond.

You could increase your awareness of contemplative, intangible things like the universe, God, the Field, nature, religion, philosophies, love, meditations or faith. A lot of quiet time mixed with pondering, imagining and seeking meaning in life results in spiritual growth. So does reading spiritual material and having discussions with spiritual people, spending time in spiritual places or adopting a philosophy or a religion. There are many ways to find spirituality.

Emotional maturity is the really difficult one, because it takes emotional maturity to admit to emotionally immaturity. We can only become emotionally stable once we have become emotionally mature. If I am emotionally immature I will feel a lot of intense feelings and react very strongly to things with my emotions instead of my common sense or logic. I would especially react to criticism, feed back or complaints. Being highly intelligent, mentally mature or learned does not exempt anyone from emotional immaturity. Taking offence easily and often keeps people trapped by prompting them to avoid or attack the very sources that would help them grow up - those willing to show them where they are being childish, non-objective or over-reactive. Being totally unwilling to be wrong, they are convinced that they are being objective and you or the others are off-track, being subjective or being childish. Over active emotional responses paralyze because the strong emotions put the body into a strong physiological condition that shuts off the mind and the intellect.

I am right, you know I am.
There's no point in denying.
My facts are indisputable.
You'd waste your time in trying.

Whatever subject you might raise,
One thing is for certain,
I'll argue on relentlessly
Until the final curtain.

I never can be wrong you see,
My ego cannot take it.
I'll forge ahead regardless,
Even if I have to fake it.

by Terri Ann Laws

To improve emotional maturity we need to take more responsibility for ourselves, our behaviour and the effect we have on others. We need to realize that we alone are in control of our experience. We choose our expectations, interpretations and retaliations. We need to stop seeing the world as happening to us, and realize that it is happening anyway, and we choose our response. We need to learn to broaden the gap between the stimuli we receive and our response to it so that we take a moment to choose an appropriate, constructive response. We need to learn to not just react immediately, charged by an emotion. We need to look less for excuses and more for reasons, less for problems and more for solutions. We need to teach ourselves to separate our emotions from the things we encounter in life. We need to learn how to feel calm and controlled by choice in any situation.

Achieving a higher degree of emotional maturity makes a huge improvement in the quality of our lives and our relationships. This is because the decision to be either happy or miserable becomes closer within our reach. Our emotional state will no longer be dependent on the way we are treated by others. We will no longer be controlled by our own rampant emotions or by other people's choices, actions and reactions to us or around us. We will no longer imagine ourselves to be helpless and at the mercy of certain people or our environment. We will no longer accuse others of causing our feelings or moods, and this will vastly improve all our interaction and effectiveness with others. We will be able to think clearly and rationally in the face of problems or conflict, or be able to ask for help when we need it.

We know we have reached emotional maturity when:

- We no longer yearn to receive love, but only to give it.
- We have no 'rules' for others, only rules for ourselves.
- We have no behavioural expectations of others, only behavioural expectations of ourselves.
- We are able to allow others to do, be, think, believe and say whatever they like to us, at us and in front of us – and be OK about it.
- We are able to choose how we would like to feel about anything.
- We can decide what mood we'd like to be in, and put ourselves into the mood of our choice by ourselves, regardless of who is doing what around us.
- We no longer respond with our emotions unless we decide to allow our emotions the freedom. The appropriate response, or an appropriate response is available to us.
- We no longer find ourselves dictated to and controlled by our emotions and we have choice about how we want to feel and how we want to respond, and we are able to feel calm under pressure or attack.
- We are able to allow others to tell the truth, their truth, or any truth, and we are able to listen objectively without needing to stop them, interrupt, defend, justify or interfere at all.
- It doesn't matter what others think or feel, and we are able to decide whether we want to have it matter to us or not.

- People no longer have the power to make us angry or hurt us no matter how hard they try.
- Our emotions belong to us and we can run them on purpose regardless of what is happening in the world around us.

Although a large amount of spiritual maturity can help us achieve emotional maturity, mental maturity cannot always help, except to help us understand that we need emotional maturity. This is evident in so many doctors who are very defensive and reactive when their patients 'question' their diagnosis or methods or ask for a second opinion. Even many psychiatrists childishly abandon patients who disagree with them or confront them or beg to be weaned off their medication. You can hold a PhD or three and still remain immature emotionally, very immature emotionally. Being ego bound, defensive and reactive is a sure sign of emotional immaturity, and even massive mental maturity does not necessarily have the slightest impact or beneficial effect on emotional maturity.

Choose the areas in life where you want to grow in maturity. Mental maturity will give you much more options and choices and enable you to achieve more dreams and goals. Emotional maturity will vastly increase the quality of your relationships, your popularity and your results. Spiritual maturity will improve your inner peace, connection and feelings of safety and belonging in the world. Good luck and may you grow and develop and evolve in ways that surprise and delight even yourself.

Winners and losers (received via email)

A loser says: It can't be done.

A winner says: Let's find a way.

A loser says: You've got a lot to learn.

A winner says: There's so much more I need to learn.

A loser says: You're wrong. I'm right.

A winner says: You're probably right, but I see it differently.

A loser says: Who do you think you are telling me that?

A winner says: Thank you for pointing that out to me.

A loser makes promises.

A winner makes commitments.

A loser tries to discredit those who are superior.

A winner learns from those who are superior.

A loser goes around a problem.

A winner goes through it.

After making a mistake, a loser says: It's not my fault.

After making a mistake a winner says: I was wrong.

Bad People

Describe a bad person. What specifically makes them 'bad'? Are there occasions when this behaviour is excusable or understandable? Why do you think a bad person is bad? What is prompting them to be like that? Do they see themselves as bad? Do they admit that what they did was bad or do they try to justify it?

So who is really bad we ask,
since we all think we're good.
We know the reasons why we do,
what we think we should.

Yet actually, against the light,
without those reasons why,
They're wicked things within themselves,
and to ourselves we lie.

So how can we be saved? We ask,
to happy peace and truth
When all we have is what we are,
and that we did not choose?

We didn't know the choice was ours,
until we have been shown.
Tis only after sin and pain,
we realize we have grown.

We do our best to justice serve
and put the world to rights.
Inflicting pain and misery
and justly scold and fight.

I've never met a human yet,
who openly agrees

defending and justifying ourselves, we will never be able to admit to our own imperfections or wrong choices. As long as we refuse to admit we were wrong, we cannot choose otherwise in future. And the things that go wrong in our lives will continue to go wrong.

Nothing around us will change until we make a few changes to ourselves. Accusing others of being bad and expecting them to change is often a pointless and futile route, because those others may not agree that they are bad, and they may not want to change. We do not have the right or the power to change everyone else. We do not really have the right to judge anyone else. Trying to change others only alienates us from them and causes huge, negative conflicts. We can only change ourselves. If we want anything or anyone around us to change we first have to change ourselves. Very often, this actually causes others around us to change because they begin responding to the different person we have become instead of the person we used to be.

If someone has done something 'wrong', it only means it's not what you wanted them to do, or what you thought was 'right'. Every behaviour is 'right' in some context. This includes premeditated mass murder – if you are a soldier sent out to war. Wrong only means 'It's not what I want, it's not working for me.'

As one woman said so beautifully to me,

> ".... I have decided to stop insulting my teenagers because I have found that it is not working as I wanted it to. At first I argued with them and insisted that I was not insulting them, I was mentioning indisputable, provable facts and pointing out the things they were doing wrong and

the negative traits they have that want changing. They pointed out to me that to them these 'facts' were insults, and that if they were to say those things to me, I would indeed call them insults. I listened to them with an open mind (difficult as that was) and eventually saw their point. I thought I was pointing out wrongs that needed to be righted, but they received this as character assassinations and insults. By me seeing them as bad, they were seeing me as bad.

I had hoped that pointing out their shortcomings to them would cause them to admit, and see the error of their ways. I expected them to change their behaviour and character for the better. I found instead that they become more sullen, uncooperative and difficult. From these observations, I deduce that insulting my teenagers - for me at least - is 'wrong' because it's not working for me or them. It in fact alienates my teenagers from me and puts us in separate enemy camps and reduces the amount of cooperation I get from them. Also, I can see now that it causes them to have less confidence and less self-esteem than some of their peers. Pointing out their faults does not result in them changing their ways, it only results in them losing confidence, hope, self esteem and also it turns them into my enemies."

I couldn't have put it better. This is so true, and it is true of any close relationship where someone takes it upon themselves to correct another.

When things aren't working, most people try the same thing harder. When I began examining my life more closely, I found I was doing quite a lot of things 'wrong'. The only reason I call them wrong now is because they were not working for me. They were causing me all kinds of problems. I didn't want the problems they were causing me. As I examined my choices and behaviour and the actual results I was getting, I got a clear, objective view. This allowed me to notice that what I was doing was not going to work and had never worked, and so I was able to decide to try something else instead - and see if perhaps that reaped better consequences for me and for everyone else.

You might find that being at peace with all mankind works far better than having enemies, or people out there who you believe are bad, or people who believe that you have harmed them in some way. This is because most people want to get even or blacken your name when they are upset with you. Getting even, being nasty or selfish, dishonest or thoughtless does not work, even if and even when others fully deserve it. It generally just causes us to play torturous negative mental 'movies' and thoughts in our heads.

It also causes fear, suspicion and insecurity when we start thinking, 'If I can do that to them, then they can do that to me.' It is far safer and more peaceful to simply not make enemies with anyone. When we take it upon ourselves to judge others and do 'justice', we do even more damage to ourselves than we do to the world out there. And everything we do comes back to us and contributes to creating our lives.

Taking full responsibility for all the consequences we cause and the consequences we suffer affords us a whole lot more control over our lives and our happiness. We are then no longer a helpless victim of other people's choices, words or behaviour. We can change so much of the 'badness' we have been receiving from others simply by seeing things differently, and changing our own perceptions. This will change our behaviour, choices and attitude, and therefore their next response to us. We can dismantle a feud even before it begins by allowing and detaching and practising non-judgement. Other people always have their reasons for the things they do, even when they do really 'bad' things. In their mind it is the right thing, or the only thing, or they have no choice. That is what they are seeing, thinking or feeling.

When we see someone else as 'bad', we get a flood of awful emotions. These emotions can ruin our day. People can become almost obsessed with setting someone straight or exposing the error of someone's ways. This does little to stop the 'bad' person, but lots instead to create misery in the 'judge'. Why lie awake at night worrying or mulling over the shocking injustice or wrongness of something or someone? The person that eventually ends up doing all the suffering is the judge - not the 'wrong doer'. The enemy actually really lies only within

I asked the Guru

Why is it that I am the one who suffers when others have wronged me? Surely the guilty one, the perpetrator should be the one to suffer all the torment and pain? I can find neither justice nor comfort for my hurt and anger. Now even my friends and loved ones are beginning to turn from me.

And he replied

The enemy lies within. Your struggle with mankind is an illusion. You will conquer your enemy by learning all there is to know about him. He exists within the walls of your own castle.

Your castle is made up of your understanding, thoughts, memories, words, actions and achievements, also your feelings, opinions, your relationships and your body. This is the monument that is you, which you present to the world. The world reacts to you according to the way that you present yourself to it.

What is the point of making a hostile plundering against life when we are all part of each other's experience? If I selfishly take for myself, I alienate myself physically and emotionally. People are a part of my environment. If I hurt people I hurt my environment. I have to live in my environment and therefore I hurt myself.

I am a part of everyone I ever meet or know and they are a part of me because once I know them, they exist in my experience. They can never leave. It is not given to man to remove any part of his memory. People are only actors on my stage and it is I who assign them each a role of importance or insignificance according to my choice. If I hate them, the image of them and their deeds in my head hurts me. The hate and the consequential pain grows in me, not in them.

Whatever I do against them, no matter how justified, collects on my karma. We cannot justify ourselves. If we could, then there would be no police, no courts of law and no prisons, for every man can explain with good reasons for doing the things he does. We do not have the capacity to be fair because we will always judge ourselves by our intentions, but we judge others by their actions. We cannot select our own jury because we will select all those who are kindly disposed towards us. Therefore only those whom we have wronged can justify us - if they will. Only we can justify those who have wronged us - if we will.

But why should we?

Because we only hurt ourselves if we don't. When we accuse others and find them guilty of doing us wrong, we multiply the damage that they have done to us. Every time we replay the movie, we hurt all over again. We reaffirm, practise and entrench the bad. Do not chase after the poisonous snake that bites you. Rather take immediate steps to get the poison out. If a bee stings you, do you plot hatred and revenge against it for many months? Do you seek to have that particular bee punished? The enemy exists only in our interpretation and understanding. Bad things happen by the hand of fate, the hand of nature and the hand of man. This does not make them enemies. The only real enemy lies within.

Perhaps you have unwittingly punished your friends and loved ones by attempting to extract comfort and compassion from them for yourself in your hour of grief. Perhaps you have brought them all your poison when you should have been bringing them your joy and your love. This too carries its own consequences. It is obvious that they would soon grow weary of you. Wouldn't you? How can you expect them to be good company for you when you have been such dismal company for them? Surely if I want happiness in my life I must first be willing to give it before I can expect to receive it.

I see my error now. What shall I do?

Practise divine compassion, detachment and freedom from selfishness and ego. Recover quickly from wrongs and bare no grudge or malice. Always be of good cheer and see the funny side of everything so that you may practise laughter and joy, for this is indeed the best medicine. Find endless delight in the most ordinary things and go through life like a fascinated tourist with plenty a joyful story to tell. This will earn for you all the love and comfort you need.

Thank you Guru, I have found the enemy, he lies within and I will kill him with kindness

It is not possible for anyone to do anything wrong without first having reasons to believe it is right.

Our senses are continually picking up raw data from the world around us. Our eyes see, our ears hear, we touch, feel, taste and smell. All this data is absolutely useless to us until we have recognized it, understood it, categorized it and given it meaning. The raw data by itself is meaningless. In order to function in the world and interact with it, we need to assign everything relevance, importance and meaning. The meaning we give determines our response or reaction.

For example, once we have understood certain words from people to be insulting, we are thereafter insulted by those words. Once we understand certain actions to be threatening, we thereafter feel compelled to protect or defend ourselves from those kinds of actions. Our bodies respond with various sensations to the thoughts that our minds produce. These sensations compel us to action. The actions we take depend on what we understand the raw data to mean.

This becomes a significantly useful observation when trying to understand why people do what they do, especially if they are doing things that we interpret as destructive or wrong. Every human being can confidently defend, explain and justify every single thing that he does. There is always a reason, even if he has created the reason and convinced himself of it. Sometimes the reason is unacceptable to many others, but always the reason is acceptable to those people who think and feel the way the 'wrongdoer' does. It stands to reason therefore that everyone is always doing what he or she believes to be the right thing, or the only thing or the best they can do under the circumstances – as they see it.

We are always trying to survive, help, see justice done, get even, save someone, save ourselves, fix things, or change things. We evaluate whatever happens according to our understanding, our rules and values, and then we decide what to do about it. Sometimes people do not have clear untarnished judgement. Sometimes people do not look carefully at long-term consequences. Sometimes people don't even consider consequences at all. Sometimes people are so deeply into reaction, emotion or panic that they are not even able to consider the cost to others or the consequences.

Sometimes people lack the resources or skills to choose otherwise and don't realize that more resources or help are available to them. Sometimes people misunderstand or misrepresent what has happened and therefore respond inappropriately. Then there are times when people are driven by such powerful emotions that thought of any kind is not possible, for example; road rage, fear, deep loss.

Whatever we believe to be true is true, because it is real and true to us. Everyone can find others who will agree with him. The way we see the world, the way we interpret what others do, determines how we choose to respond. Since it is not possible for anyone to do anything 'wrong' (because we are all doing what we believe to be the best at the time under the circumstances as we see it) the way to change 'wrong' or 'bad' behaviour is to fully understand the reasoning behind the choosing of it, and find a constructive way to stop it immediately in the most intelligent and mature way. Only with a really clear understanding of why it seemed necessary to that person to behave that way can we think up ways to prevent repeat performances.

Working with the wrong doer and helping him/her find more effective ways to meet their objectives is far more effective, successful and lasting than punishment, rejection or rebuke. If you are on their side and genuinely want to help them get their own way in a more acceptable and agreeable fashion, they'll let you help them. You can only influence people if you are willing to understand them, agree with them, empathize with them and help them. If you are willing do this, you can persuade them to make better choices in future. You can then help them see why better choices will be in their own best interests. This way you can put a stop to the wrong and bad while at the same time building good and cooperative relationships with the doers. This will afford you real power, authority and influence, which is not challenged or resisted.

This is the reason why prisons, police and the justice system has always failed to reduce the crime rate. Most criminals come out of jail much better educated in the ways of crime and are far less likely to get caught next time, and their bitterness at having been put in jail gives them powerful motivations to go out and do much worse. When one man judges another to be wrong, a great wrong is created by the judge. The 'crime' still exists in the one judged, and now - as he is rejected and punished - resentment, hatred and other pain is added to him as well. Criminals very seldom rehabilitate, because the reasons they did what they did are very valid and real to them. Given the same set of circumstances again, they would do the same thing again.

It is far more constructive to remove the crime from the criminal by teaching him new and more effective ways of getting what he wants and needs in future. If it was money he needed, teach him business skills. If it was revenge he wanted, teach him some of the kinds of skills you are learning from this book. If it was hatred, then help him to heal his heart. If he was afraid, teach him how to feel safe in the world. If he was bitter and alone, teach him how to find love in the world. Solve the problem and cure the cause instead of punishing the person and society will evolve to a better and safer place for everyone.

If we heal the problem from inside, then the person will not choose to do crime again. If we judge them, hate them and punish them, they will do far worse crimes in future and they are less likely to get caught the next time. Prisons will always teach the inmates many more 'criminal' skills than they came in with, and the harsh treatments they get from offices and wardens, and nasty types they meet in prison, hurt and embitter new inmates even more and make them very much worse when they come out than they were when first they went in. Criminals generally have even less conscience when they come out.

Crime is not the problem. Society's hatred, rejection and judgement of its citizens is the problem. Only those who have suffered a tremendous amount of pain in life feel compelled to commit a crime. Crime is a result of massive pain, lack of resources and various ill treatments, neglect and suffering. Crime is created by society, and it can be stopped if all society takes responsibility for creating it, and determines to heal the hearts that do the crime.

Instead of punishing the person, find the real reason and help the person to make better choices in future. 'Good' people do terrible things to people they are assume are 'bad'. Ask any school child to give you a list of awful, cruel, nasty things their teachers have done to some of the kids recently and you'll get an enthusiastic long list. Do you think the teachers believe they did wrong to the kids? Of course not! The teacher is likely to believe herself (or himself) to be the victim or the bringer of right and justice. So who decides what is evil, cruel, wrong or bad? And having made that assessment, who dishes out the 'appropriate' punishment or correction?

Education, compassion and social responsibility are the solutions, not 'justice'. Justice is really only revenge. We commit crimes of revenge against the people we believe are bad, and against criminals and then wonder why they don't change their ways? There is no such thing as a bad person, only a person who is hurt, embittered, insane, confused or desperate. If we work on the real problem and not on the fruits of the problem, we will go a long way towards solving it. Evil begets evil and evil is nothing more than some person's interpretation. Everyone is evil and everyone is good, and it is only in our judgements and punishments and attempts to correct the evil we think we see that creates evil in the first place.

The police, lawyers and justice system create crime, and that is why all ancient societies living on the planet today do not have crime. The Koi San tribe in the Kalahari desert, the Intuits in the North pole regions, the wild men in Borneo and all the other ancient tribes on the planet today do not have crime because they do not have police, lawyers, prisons and concepts of evil within their own societies. Parents don't see children as 'bad' and therefore don't instil badness in their children. Teachers don't see children as 'bad' and therefore don't look to correct or punish any. Society doesn't see any of its citizens as 'bad' and therefore doesn't set about putting a stop to what is not there. Each incident is dealt with by the elders then and there, assuming the 'bad' act came as a result of some reason and they get to the bottom of it together and solve the problem.

Perhaps one day we will all actually begin to be as civilized as the ancient cultures are.

The Art of Listening

I can listen to you on many different levels:

1. I can listen to your actual words, and hear the context. There is no meaning intended other than the words. Example - news or information.

2. I can listen to your actual words, and feel the context. Example - I feel sorry for you as you speak because you are sad when telling me about what happened to you. Or while hearing your opinion that is different from mine, I might feel frustrated.

3. I can listen for your meaning, or what I think your meaning is, paying less attention to your actual words. Example - you are beating around the bush or being long winded or speaking in a way I don't fully relate to.

4. I can half listen, paying no real attention to either your words or your meaning. Example – I find the

subject mundane, or you're jabbering away while I am busy, or tolerating someone's child chattering away about school and friends.

5. I can pretend to listen. I can perhaps even say 'aha' now and then so you think I'm listening. I'm probably thinking about something else in my mind. I could be far away. Example - A husband sitting with the news paper or with the radio on while his wife jabbers, or I'm busy typing while you speak to me, or I'm at a boring presentation.

6. I can refuse to listen. I can stare at you as though I'm listening, saying in my mind 'What rubbish!' Example - you are trying to convince me of something, or trying to convert me, or I think you're creating reasons and justifications or excuses.

7. I can listen with no intent to understand, but every intention of replying as soon as possible. I make no effort to give you a hearing, I'm just itching to start speaking myself. Example - Something you said reminds me of something I want to say. Your words trigger my story and I'm trying to remember what I want to say as soon as I get a gap.

8. I can listen to your words and your meaning and try to understand what you mean by what you say. I am making an effort to listen to you and to understand you, but only in so far as it affects me. My intention is still to react. I'm really only interested in how your words or feelings affect me, or how they affect our relationship or my agenda. Example - In a relationship, I know what I mean when I say that, but what do you mean when you say that? What are

215

you trying to tell me? (I love you but...) Or in a negotiation, when one side listens intensely only because they want lots of information so they can use it to gain the upper hand.

9. I can listen to you. I can listen with every intention of understanding exactly what you mean by what you say and how it affects you - not me. I want to understand what you are trying to tell me. I try to understand where you are coming from. I try to understand you and your world for your sake. I try to understand your feelings and your experience without wondering how that affects me. I'm wondering how it affects you. I have no intention of reacting, expecting or judging. I have no agenda, just an open, genuine heart.

Number 9 is the true art of listening. This is how I can listen artfully to you. To do this I must really want to know what and how you are feeling because I want to understand you as a person. I want you to express yourself fully without fear of how I might take it. I honestly want to know the whole truth of how you really think and feel. I honour the trust you are placing in me. I don't place any moral judgements on anything you say. I completely allow you your opinion. You can say things that are off track, bad manners, untrue, accusatory or anything. It is the truth according to you, and I want to know it because I want to know you, even if it insults me, falsely accuses me or makes me look or feel bad.

My intention is not to catch you out, prove you wrong, set you straight or correct you. My intention is not to defend my own position, ego or reputation. My intention is not to decide whether you deserve to stay in my good books or not. I'm not trying to assess your loyalty. I realize that if I do any of these things, it would be at the expense of you opening up to me, and you may never trust me again. I need you to open up to me in order for me to really be able to understand you on a deeper and more intimate level, to understand how your mind works, how your heart works, to really understand your experience from your perspective. My intention is to know you and to know who you really are. Nothing is more important to me than that right now as I listen with the art of listening.

The art of listening gives me the opportunity to know you and understand you so well that I can build or heal our relationship all by myself without your cooperation.

If I could tell you all my fears and get it off my chest,
If I could tell you what I hate and what I love the best,
If I could fully clear the air and really speak my mind,
With total, open honesty, the truest you could find.

If I could only trust and know that all was safe to say,
If I could bear my deepest truth with nothing in the way,
If I could tell you everything with nothing left unsaid, And
tell you what is actually both in my heart and head.

Then we could get as close as ever human beings could be.
We'd reach a depth of knowing that would surely set us free.
Of all the pain and doubt and hurt that keeps our worlds
apart,
And keeps us both defensively protecting self and heart.

Intimacy is a need that human beings all crave,
But the risk is so extreme, and few are quite that brave.
We'd rather suffer endlessly this empty, hungry need,
Than suffer vulnerability, attempting this to feed.

by Terri Ann Laws

If you really feel that I have been totally selfish, I need you to tell me that. If you don't tell me, then I will never know. The fact that I don't know, will not change your opinion. As long as you hold that opinion, your behaviour towards me will reflect it. That will damage our relationship. But if I let you tell me, then at least I know. That information is extremely useful to me whether or not I decide to change anything. If I want to have any control over my relationship with you, then it is only myself I can consider changing.

Then I have the choice and it is mine to choose, then if I want to, with your help I can explain or change so that you can love and respect the real me for real. At least if I know, I will have the opportunity to earn a different feeling or opinion from you. I can find out if anyone else feels that way. I can change my behaviour. I can salvage our relationship. I don't want you to placate me or humour me. I don't want you to tell me sweet little lies for the sake of peace. I don't want you to pretend you love me. I don't want to play games. I don't want you to tell me what you think I want to hear. I want a genuine and sincere relationship based on trust and truth. And I can only get this if I let you tell me the truth without punishing you for your honesty. Punishment would include things like becoming angry or hurt or sulking or reacting in any way you won't like, because if I do that, then you would be ill advised to tell me the truth in future.

If I really want to know how you feel about me or about anything, I have a far better chance of getting the full story if I listen artfully to you. Listening to you with every intent to understand you, no intent to reply, every intent to allow, no intent to judge, every intent to be informed and no intent to condemn or to change your mind.

If I do not allow you to express your feelings, they stay inside of you secretly. They may even be smouldering. They affect the way you treat me. They affect what you think of me. You act on your feelings. All our actions are based on our feelings, thoughts and opinions. If I allow you to express your feelings, you have no need to act on them. If I allow you to express all your thoughts and opinions, then at least I know the real you, and I'm much better off knowing the real you rather than the you I think you should be, rather than the 'you' you have led me to believe is you. Then you have no need to pretend with me, be someone else to me or act out of frustration against me. Take note of this. It's very important. *Spoken feelings do not need action.*

No matter how hard I try to hide it, if I don't really want to listen to you, it will show on my face, in my attitude and my mannerisms. You will see it in my eyes. You will feel uneasy or become afraid of consequences and stop speaking or monitor your words. You will sense my duplicity and shut up.

If at any point I cannot take it anymore, I have to be honest, own up and say so. I can say, 'Please can we carry on later? I really want to hear you, but I need it in smaller doses. I would like to go and think about what you have said so far. Thank you for being honest with me.'

I must not become a victim or a martyr. I must not allow your words to bully or hurt or anger me. I must remember it is only information, important information, and it gives me choices. I must not take on guilt. I must not forget the reason I am listening to you - so that I can understand how and what you really feel. The reason I want to know and understand this is so that I can intelligently decide what to

220

do about it. I must allow you. I must allow me. I can be strong. I can be powerful. I am perfectly capable of correcting any 'wrongs' I may have unwittingly committed. (Wrong meaning 'It isn't working for you so it isn't working for me - i.e. you are not happy with me or our relationship as a result). I am perfectly free to decide not to change too if that is what I believe is best, but if I don't have the actual, real truth, then I don't have my actual, real choices.

I am perfectly capable of taking full responsibility for myself and for my behaviour and for my relationship with you. My relationship with you is a part of me, it is mine, and I want it to be a good one for my sake as much as yours.

Now that I have allowed you, I know what I'm dealing with. I understand why you do what you do. I have the thinking behind the behaviour. I know how your mind works, I know how your heart works. This is very useful information to me. I can understand why you have been - perhaps - off towards me.

I am grateful for this opportunity to get closer to you. This is an opportunity to improve our relationship and for me to avoid similar problems with you or with others at another time. I am grateful to you for showing me more about myself, aspects of me I was unaware of. I am healing you by listening to you, and healing me by learning from you, believing you and allowing you. I am growing much stronger in character by going through this. I am now in a much stronger position to build or heal all my relationships. I have something to go on. I have something to work with.

I have walked on holy ground. I have touched another human soul. I have been deeply trusted. I have honoured that trust. This means I am trustworthy. I can be trusted. I proved it. I have honour and integrity. I'm worthy of love. I feel it. I love so deeply at this moment. I really love you, and I love myself. I have earned my love and yours. Real self-love. It feels absolutely wonderful.

Here is a letter from a teenager to his parents. I wrote it for a teenager I was counselling once. He really wanted to explain to his parents how he felt, but he explained all the reasons to me why he could not do that. So I took what he had told me and put it into a letter for him to give to his parents. It worked an absolute treat.

Dear Mum and Dad,

You say you want my love, my friendship, my trust and my understanding, but you don't know me. You try to please me by giving me things and doing things for me, but those are the things you want to give. They are not the things I need and want. Yet I have to be very grateful or you get furious and insult me. That's why the more you give and do, the more guilty and miserable I feel.

I may not have the courage to tell you that I am only a Monopoly board. That's why your real money cannot buy you shares. In order for me to trust you enough to tell you who I am, I need you to give me time and let me speak, without telling me what to say or how to say it. I need you to withhold your judgements, opinions, criticisms and preconceived ideas. I need you to listen with your heart for the things I am afraid to say directly.

Remember, I am afraid. I am vulnerable. I am easily hurt, embarrassed and defensive. Also, there are so many words that I may not use, yet words are all I have. Words that will turn you instantly against me and make you storm out on me again in hurt or anger. Words that will cause you to punish me severely. I have to gingerly place carefully chosen words at your feet one sentence at a time. This is very hard for me but I am willing to try.

When I feel a little safer and tell you a little more, perhaps something personal or secret, I need you to treat what I've said with reverence. I need you to feel awe inspired by my courage, surprised by my uniqueness. I need you to take me seriously. I need you to recognise my currency as valid. If you do this, I will begin to trust you. I will be able to allow you a little closer. You will have made a huge deposit in my own unique Monopoly bank account, and you will become my valuable customer.

I am lonely. I need a customer. You say you want to come in. I want to let you in, but it is so risky. It is very hard for me to do this because you could hurt me terribly. I'll need time to see if I can really trust you. I need to test if you really have my best interests at heart. I need to make sure you are not only trying to manipulate me or gain more power over me. I need to see what you are going to do with my vulnerability once I have given it to you.

If you treasure it, I will treasure you. Your shares will go sky high. You will become my very valuable customer. My heart will sing whenever I see you, as it did when I was teeny. The more you make it safe for me to do so, the more I will open up to you, and the closer we can become. You will see that I am very different from you. If you allow me, you might find that you can respect me.

Everything in my world has a value to me in my currency. Once you know my currency, you can ask the price (value) of anything, and I will tell you. For example (please don't take offence now), you try to manipulate me with pocket money, but my dignity is more valuable to me than any carrot on any stick. Perhaps the most expensive thing in my world is not gold, but forgiveness, not diamonds but Litchis. With much love and hope,

Your Teenager.

The Art of Silence

Most people feel very uncomfortable when there is silence between them. They feel compelled to say something, fill the gap, be entertaining. It is a huge relief to allow yourself to be comfortable in silence and not feel the need to fill it with anything at all; just be in peace. So many people find silence uncomfortable that some people even use silence as a punishment with the 'silent treatment'. Yet silence can be a beautiful, amazing space to be in. To just exist in each other's company comfortably with no need for any words at all.

Silence can be so healing. If you and I have had a fall out, I can come and sit next to you, perhaps lean on your shoulder or put my arms around you and just sit or rock gently without saying a single word. Words would just get in the way. I can just be there and feel close to you. Silence is also a very useful tool to master for a lot of occasions, for example, when someone is shouting or screaming at you, if you just look at them with a loving peaceful expression and say absolutely nothing at all, they eventually stop. In fact they are unlikely to do it again if you simply don't respond in any way. Well, they might try once or twice more, but they'll soon stop if they see there is absolutely no point.

Silence is also helpful as a response when you're being asked questions you don't want to answer, or when someone is demanding information from you and you don't want to communicate with them. You can also use it when you're being accosted by a pushy salesperson. The art of this kind of silence is to maintain a loving, detached, peaceful look on your face and remain absolutely silent. It is very frustrating for the person, and they soon give up and leave you alone. It ensures you maintain your power and protect your space and your rights. You can chuckle about it afterwards.

Silence can also be used as a powerful tool to get to know someone. If I sit down next to you and say absolutely nothing for long enough, sooner or later you will start to speak. If I acknowledge you with a welcoming sound like 'hmmm', you know I'm listening, and you can carry on. If I remain silent and keep on listening, you will get deeper and deeper involved in what you are sharing with me. I'll travel with you through your story or explanation. I'll try to imagine I am you, doing and feeling the things you are describing to me. For a brief moment in time I can see what it feels like to be you.

In order to practise the art of listening, I need to learn to be silent. One cannot fully listen without fully engaging in silence. The art of silence is a prerequisite to the art of listening. The art of silence can almost turn into the sacred art of silence when it comes to relationship repairing or deep, sincere listening.

Here are some steps you can go through to remind yourself to keep your mouth and your mind completely silent:

- I have to silence my voice, Shut up and not speak at all except to express amazement with 'Wow!' or to ask for clarity – 'Please explain further.' Or to encourage you to carry on with a warm 'Hmm' or 'Uhuh.'
- I have to silence my mind of my own home movie. I cannot be thinking about my similar experiences

while you are talking. I need to be trying to get into your experience as if I were you, not me.

- I have to silence my mind of my own excuses, reasons, and justifications. I may not express them, but I may not think them either.

- I have to silence my opinions. I must silence my internal running commentary. I may not think to myself while you are talking, 'You may feel that way, but I certainly don't.' 'you only feel that way because you are ...' 'You don't understand me (or it)' 'I could tell you a few things that would change your mind.' I may not run opinions or commentary or 'mental noise' of any sort.

- I have to silence my ego. I may not be thinking to myself, 'After all I've done for you!' 'Now I know what you think of me!' 'Who do you think you are?' 'How dare you insult me like that!' I may not indulge my feelings and emotions because I need mine still in order to feel yours.

- I have to silence my self-pity. Feeling sorry for myself puts a burden or a guilt trip on you. It is also total indulgence and very immature. It is a weakness. It is destructive, it can never be constructive. It would be not facing facts. It would be being a victim 'wishing' things were different. The look on my face will give me away if I am feeling self-pity.

- I have to silence my judgement of you. I must not condemn you. For example; 'You are a miserable person.' 'You are so narrow minded.' 'You are emotionally immature.' 'I thought you were stronger than that.' And other such judgements.

In order to master the art of listening, we need to master the art of being silent. All it takes is practice. This is one skill anyone can learn. Yes, it may be hard at first, but it quickly grows easy and it then grows us into hugely special and mature people. It is one of the biggest strength, power and character-growing tools there are and it enables us to learn masses about another person. Learning the art of listening gives us a major edge. We can learn from other people's experiences as well as from our own. We can always find out exactly where we stand, exactly who we are to others, what to do and how to approach things and people, to get the best long-term benefits for all. It makes available to us a lot of very useful data about others and about people in general. It puts us streets ahead.

Most importantly, we can get very, very close to people. The closer we get to others, the closer we get to ourselves. The safer we feel getting closer to others, the safer we feel getting closer to what is deep inside ourselves. The better we get to know others, the better we get to know ourselves. Because the safer others feel with us, the safer we feel with ourselves. This has the delightful result of affording us a feeling of total safety in the world.

The more we see what makes others tick, the more 'ways to tick' we learn about. We find our own way in the midst of discovering others. When others trust us, we trust ourselves because we see we are trustworthy. This makes us feel very safe and welcome in the world. This is a major repair kit and antidote for loneliness, isolation and alienation. It is also a powerful repair kit for healing relationships.

Meditation

Meditation is the art of silencing the mind. Taking a break from all the thinking and pondering and plotting, analysing, scheming and planning we have to do all day. Our thinking can leave us just as exhausted as our activities can. Giving the mind a rest now and then aids clarity of thought. It helps us make better decisions and helps us to stay focused. Being able to clear the mind of all thoughts makes it possible for to us to stop in our tracks and change our thoughts. Thought control enables us to choose happy, constructive thoughts and reject negative ones. Meditation helps us gain control over our mind so that it will obey us, and then we can effectively use the art of attraction and deliberately create our own destiny. You can stop your thoughts and you can watch your thoughts and can laugh at your thoughts. Practicing meditation makes this possible.

Learning to meditate

There are many types of meditation and many ways to meditate apart from the way I'll describe here. You can try this one or you can find another one that you like. Consult any esoteric or new age magazine, and you'll find many adverts to do with meditation and learning the art.

Stop the mind. Clear your mind of all thoughts and concentrate on one pictured object, like a coin or a leaf or a rose. Think of nothing else for five minutes. When any thought comes into your mind, send it away kindly and gently and tell it to wait till later. Remind yourself you're concentrating on the one picture. Keep your mind empty except for the picture for two minutes. After a few days gradually begin increasing the time to five minutes, then ten minutes of stopping the mind. Do this mediation at least once every day, and twice or three times a day will be even better.

If you prefer words to pictures, then repeat an affirmation or mantra over and over, concentrating on the exact words only and nothing else. Use exactly the same affirmation for a week before changing it. Some people find it hard at first, and if you turn out to be one of these, don't just give up because the good news is that those who put the most effort in initially find they are much better at it eventually. Breathing slowly, deeply and regularly also helps to keep the mind occupied while you meditate and accelerates your progress. You will be delightfully surprised at how easy it is to find peace of mind when you meditate regularly. All kinds of problems just seem to disappear on their own like magic, and no one knows exactly why. It just is.

Other ways that meditation helps

- It makes detaching easier, especially when you're noticing yourself wanting to react.
- It takes you out of a speed wobble.
- It relaxes you when you are getting tense about something.
- It helps you feel calmer.
- It helps you gather yourself before facing a conflict or stressful situation so that you manage it effectively.
- You'll sleep better at night when you are able to clear your mind of rushing thoughts because it's rushing thoughts that usually keep us awake.
- After a mental break you are able to get a more objective view, because all the clutter is removed.

- It is necessary for the art of attracting because it gives you more control over what you absentmindedly think about all the time.
- It makes sleep more restful and brings nicer dreams.
- It increases your good luck for some unexplainable reason.
- It improves health and wellbeing and rapidly accelerates healing.
- It improves memory and concentration.

You could take up transcendental meditation or join some or other group that meditates. There are many ways to learn to meditate, and the benefits of meditation are enormous.

Communication

There are at least five different levels at which people communicate.

I may be completely closed and share nothing of myself, or I can be completely open on all levels and enjoy real meaningful communication with people. A lot depends on my intrinsic sense of my own value. Being full of my own agenda or having a fear of rejection or ridicule could interfere with my communication. I need to feel some degree of trust or safety before I can open up to you and before I can allow you to open up to me.

When we open up to another, we reveal ourselves and tell them who we are, and this is a risk. Being accepted or rejected depends largely on what we say.

Depending on the degree of safety one person feels with the other, there are five levels of communicating.

Level 1: This is very closed and unwilling to communicate. Recognized by the use of nothing other than common polite phrases, uttered as a programmed response to being spoken to. They politely acknowledge whatever you say with words such as 'Fine thank you and how are you?' but say nothing back except perhaps the occasional common phrase or cliché, and everything they say really means nothing. If I only communicate on this level, then no one will ever know anything about me and my own feelings or ideas. I remain a stranger to everyone.

Level 2: People communicating on this level reveal very little of themselves, and not enough for you to get to know them. They might add a general opinion or two such as 'Nice weather we are having, isn't it?' You might agree or disagree, but the matter is not important enough to them for them to feel vulnerable by your opinion. This is very often the testing level when we meet someone new. They might mention something that is common knowledge or recent news or obvious fact since there is no risk there at all. Whether you agree or disagree is of no consequence because it is external information, so they don't mind. These people avoid saying a word about themselves or their feelings or opinions, but they might get into a conversation with you as long as it remains shallow and common knowledge, or they will let you do most of the talking.

Level 3: I take a slightly bigger risk. I mention some opinions that I hold that are a bit more important to me. I take a chance at telling you a bit about myself and what I think. I risk rejection or a bad reaction from you, so I say something and then carefully check what you do with it. I'll tell you a little bit of something that is uniquely me. For example I might tell you that I am a Christian or an atheist

233

or I might tell you that I'm a vegetarian or I don't like sport. I am taking a risk but if you were to strongly disagree or disapprove, I can always change the subject. On this level I can wait for you to bring up a subject and then talk about that – letting you lead and sharing only my thoughts and opinions on your subject. If I get a bad reaction from you, if you reject me or argue with me, I might shut up and go back to level one or two communication with you. Level three is where most of us keep our casual acquaintances and work colleagues. Some people never communicate past level three with anyone.

Level 4: I am chatting freely and happily with you. I have forgotten my caution and I am relaxed in your company. I'll defend my point of view, I'll confidently disagree with you and I'll tell you what I think about things and I'll tell you about me. You will most likely be happy to chat back to me. This is the level at which most of us communicate with the people we know very well, such as our close friends, family and loved ones. We have a lot to share, a lot to say and we get to know each other well. We can disagree and debate and it won't result in rejection. The trust level is sufficient to allow freedom of expression and we'll chat away on any subject uncensored. But, we could get even closer to someone special - if we dare.

Level 5: This is a very special level. On this level I am willing to disclose my deepest feelings to you. I completely trust you with my private secrets. The trust level between us has to run very deep because I take major risks giving you very personal information about me, which makes me totally vulnerable.

Very few people get this close to another person. Some couples who have been married for twenty years or more have never shared many of their deepest feelings, fears, insecurities and fantasies with each other. Although we take a very big risk when we share this part of ourselves with another, we also show them our total confidence in them. We have to trust the other really well before we make ourselves this vulnerable. We can never take back anything we've said once we have said it.

The difference between a shallow, meaningless, semi-lonely existence and a rich, warm, happy life, often lies in our ability or willingness to really communicate. If you are stuck in level one or two, you will probably feel isolated, alienated and alone a lot of the time, even in company. You'll be living in your own little world even in the midst of other people. This can be a lonely place, unless you are a dreamer who likes to live in your own private world. The closer we can get to other human beings, the more often we will feel happy, loved and accepted. We experience a feeling of belonging and feel wanted and important. Few things are more enjoyable that great conversations with people we like.

If you can learn to communicate on level five with at least one person, you will experience a huge increase in inner joy and freedom. But you must both honour the trust you are placing in each other, and this will result in you remaining intimately close friends forever. This kind of trust creates precious bonds.

Those who only communicate on level one or two often feel that they have been rejected by the world, but in truth it is they who have rejected the world. Fear of rejection keeps them stuck, but it is only in risking rejection that they can ever get out of this rut. We all suffer rejection by various people at various times in our lives. This is natural. It is unreasonable to expect everyone to like us, especially since there are people that we don't like. We should be brave enough to search for friends, and then brave enough to get a little closer to them. We should risk the pain of rejection because the pain of aloneness, loneliness or isolation is worse.

Coping with rejection

We can teach ourselves to accept rejection as a normal and perfectly acceptable part of life. Imagine little children in the playground. One child comes running happily up to another and says, 'Can I play with you?' the other child says, 'NO' and pulls a face and turns her back. The first child pulls a tongue and walks off, and within three seconds has found something else to do, she's climbing up the slide. Little kids forget within seconds and hold on to nothing. Adults can do exactly the same. Having intense neurological feelings in response to rejection is ridiculous. People either do want to 'play' with you they don't. So what! It's their stuff not yours. It's their loss not yours. It's their mistake not yours. It's their problem not yours.

Create something to constantly repeat to yourself internally at any time you think you might suffer rejection of any kind. In fact repeat it at any time at all, and even ten times daily if you need to. Create a mantra or affirmation for yourself along the following lines:

- What you think of me is none of my business because I am created in the image of God by God and that makes me perfect, perfectly learning more and more about how to be my perfect self, just like you are.

- I am a child of the universe with as much right to be here as you and if you love me, I love you and if you dislike me, I dislike you and that is your loss not mine.
- All human beings are created equal and all have free will to do, to be and to enjoy whatever they choose and no one may choose what someone else should do, be or enjoy.
- You have my full permission to accept me or reject me just as I have my full permission to accept or reject you and your response to me or anything else is your stuff not mine.
- I love myself just as I am and I learn and grow every day and I don't need anyone else to approve of me because I'm capable of approving of myself and being what I want to be. No one has the right to expect me to be what they want me to be.
- I face all challenges fearlessly. All experience is useful. I am learning more and more to find joy, beauty and fascination in every experience, good or bad.
- I can never get a six unless I'm willing to throw the dice, and I hope for a six every time, but am perfectly happy to keep throwing when I get something else.

One of the above might seem just perfect for you, or you might want to use these as ideas and guidelines to create one for yourself. Make one short and simple like the seven examples above and learn it off by heart. You only need one, not seven. This will enable you to be totally immune to rejection, and then you'll be free to walk up to anyone and start a conversation and communicate with them. You can choose to begin on level one for safety, then move to level two and onwards to level four only with those individuals you feel an affinity with and want to make friends with. All other people remain friendly acquaintances at level two or three until you let them closer, and you remember that they have the same rights to accept or reject as you do.

Chatterboxes

Some people talk a lot, but they never listen. There are two types really, the loudmouth, and the chatterbox who does not know how to stop talking. For both types, talking seems to be a smoke screen that they hide behind. They use a lot of words, but there is no real two-way conversation ever going on with whoever they are talking to. They do all the talking and no one else gets a word in. It is a way of controlling people or situations. There are various feelings that motivate the 'smoke screen' talker. I have identified three:

1. They feel if they are not in control, they may be out of control.

2. They feel compelled to tell everyone who they are in case anyone notices for themselves and draws their own conclusions. They describe themselves as the person they want you to think they are. This is motivated by a conviction that if others were left to judge for themselves, they would not judge favourably.

3. They want attention, all the attention. Some are clowns, some are morbid, some are self-important, some are braggers, some whine about their childhood wounds and some are dominating or

argumentative - wanting to portray intelligence or great knowledge or power, and some complain about how miserable life is or about their life situation at you for hours, draining the life out of you.

Some smoke screen talkers often exaggerate, stretch or invent the truth. They are often unaware of the fact that they are doing this. They convince themselves that what they say is true, yet at a deeper level, I believe they do realize they are not being entirely honest, if not blatantly dishonest. They usually respond very badly (sometimes aggressively) to being challenged on any point. They want you to believe them, to be impressed and to give them your full attention. It is like some kind of compulsion they have.

Nonverbal communication

Communication goes further than words. I can tell you that I like you just by giving you a certain look for a second, and you will immediately get my message loud and clear. I can tell you I dislike you just as efficiently with a very different look. Our eyes, facial expression, posture, mannerisms and tone of voice can communicate quite convincingly. We use our hands to send signals too, sometimes unconsciously. Even our stance, our feet (tapping or rolling) and our whole bodies can communicate quite strongly without words. Even whether you are tense or relaxed communicates and gives information about you.

Non-verbal communication tells us far more about each other than words do. We can roughly tell how a person is responding to us by watching them rather than listening to them. The problem here is that we can be wrong. We can jump to conclusions based on what we interpret a certain look or gesture or body language to mean. The art and skill of interpreting other people's body language and behavioural responses can be learned. There is a whole field of study on this subject, and even that is not completely accurate because people learn certain conditioned responses from others. For example, some people fold their arms because everyone in the home where they grew up did that all the time. Never assume you know and jump to conclusions unless you've had specific training. Thinking you know what other people think or means is 'mind reading' and hallucinating and it can get you into a lot of trouble is you guess wrong.

Before you've had specific training in this field, I'll give you certain rough guidelines to guess if the person you're talking to actually wants to be there talking to you.

- If you are both doing equal amounts of the talking, or if the other is doing all the talking and you are enjoying it, then all is well. If you are doing most of the talking, then that is an alarm bell.
- If the person is smiling and nodding, laughing at your jokes or in other ways responding quite clearly as if they are enjoying themselves, then all is well.
- If the other person has lost all colour in their face, are visibly drooping and have a sick, fake, polite grin, or they look increasingly tiered that is an alarm bell. Leave them alone as soon as possible.
- If the person's pupils have dilated, their lips gone fuller, their face increased in colour, their posture become more upright and they are leaning in towards you, this is a very good sign.

But, in the long run, since words can be even more misleading than non-verbal communication, I would take the whole package and check on both to guess if communication is happening two ways. At the end of the day, unless or until we are willing to really listen to and get close to someone, establish trust and then ask them, all we have to go by is guess work and feedback.

There are times when it is important to tell people information, or to re-build a relationship or to politely complain about something you don't want, or to communicate with a loved one, subordinate, or other important person, and you really need the communication to accepted, to be listened to, understood and to be taken constructively. The skills of communicating effectively without confusion or misunderstanding include:

1. Clearly 'own' your messages by using the first person singular pronoun. Speak for yourself. Don't speak for others. Speaking for yourself means you start your sentences with 'I', not with 'you', 'we' or 'one'.

2. Ask more questions and make fewer statements. Listen to the answers you get. Listen twice as much as you speak.

3. Make your messages complete and specific. Use clear and complete statements including all the necessary information, but not including information the other already has.

4. Make your verbal and non-verbal messages congruent. Your words must match your expressions, body language, tone of voice etc, if you want to be understood. People are inclined to pay more attention to the non-verbal message than the words.

5. Don't assume a lot of what you want to say is obvious. Don't pre-suppose. Ask a few questions before you begin, to establish where the listener is and how much they already know. Then say everything you need to and sometimes you may have to say it twice.

6. Ask for feedback concerning the way your message is being received. Make sure it was understood the way you intended it to be. If it was misunderstood it is your fault not their fault.

7. Adapt your message to make it appropriate to the receiver's frame of reference.

8. Describe your feelings clearly and unambiguously. If you are feeling annoyed, say so.

9. Describe other people's behaviour without evaluating, assuming, judging or interpreting. Describe what they actually did, not what you think they intended, thought or felt. Assuming you know what they intended, thought or felt is annoying because it can be inaccurate, misleading and judgemental.

10. People are almost always thinking, 'What's in this for me?' Make sure what you are saying is something the other person is interested in hearing. If they see no benefit in it for themselves, they stop listening.

11. Match the other and establish rapport. Communication is more free and open between people who are similar in many ways. Therefore, if you want free flowing communication with someone, it pays to make an effort to get onto their wavelength. For example, if they are quiet and

withdrawn and you are being loud and extrovert, they probably won't listen to you because they won't feel comfortable with you. Be quiet and extrovert just for this discussion so they'll find it easier to hear you.

12. Become acutely sensitive to how your communication is being received. For example, don't babble on when the listener is quite clearly showing signs of discomfort. Be considerate and aware of the effect you are having.

What's going on inside?

When interacting with others, we first receive information through our senses – sight, hearing, etc.. Then we recognise it and decide what that information means, based on our prior experience and knowledge. Then we decide what we think the meaning is behind it. In this process, we make a lot of assumptions about whether it's good or bad, right or wrong, based on our own understanding and perspective.

Then we have feelings and thoughts based on our assumptions. Then we have intentions - we decide what to do. Then we express them - we do or say something based on all the above steps. Our own assumptions, understanding, conclusions and perspective cause our reactions to the information we receive through our senses. We do not react to what happens, we react to our interpretation of what happens. We do not reply to what people say, we reply to what we believe they meant.

Mind Reading

It is important to remember that we cannot possibly know what another is thinking, intending or feeling unless they tell us. It is a common mistake to assume we know the motivations, thoughts, intentions and inside workings of another. Mind reading is assuming you know what other people think, feel or intend. It is interpreting what other people say or do, and coming up with our own reasons why they said or did it and assuming our reasons are their reasons. We do this according to our own understanding of the words they use or their behaviour. What we are actually doing is describing ourselves and what we would be thinking, intending or feeling if we did or said that. We look inside ourselves and think we see others.

Such assumptions often lead us into trouble. They also prevent us from understanding others. We think we understand others because we think we understand ourselves! Even identical twins are different, so assuming you know what your teenager is going through just because you were once a teenager is foolishness. Just because you too have lost a loved one does not mean you know what your friend is going through when they lose a loved one. The dynamics of their relationship with their loved one were probably very different from yours. What is important to your teenager is very different to what was important to you when you were one. Each person is uniquely different and no two people feel exactly the same way about anything.

Be sensitive and practise the art of listening and the art of silence. It will help you to get really close to others, to find out what others think and feel, and in the process, help you find out who you are. This is a precious and valuable gift you can give to yourself. It will go a long way in helping you to become an expert communicator and eventually you'll be able to have any kind of discussion with anyone and have it go more or less the way you hoped or intended.

May your communications take on a whole new, delightful and even more constructively beneficial meaning.

Interpersonal Effectiveness

Most of our life we are interacting with others on some level or another. We have to interact with sales staff in shops, bus drivers or petrol attendants, receptionists, bank staff, neighbours, associates, our boss and our friends. The list is endless. Even a little encounter with a till operator in a café has the ability to completely ruin our day. The response we get from others can have a powerful impact on the quality of our lives.

Having a huge amount of technical skill can never compensate for a lack of interpersonal skills in our job. No matter how skilled, efficient, fast and accurate we are, if we upset everyone else all the time we will be seen as a problem instead of an asset to the company. If people don't like you they won't easily recognize your efforts or promote you. This is a natural flaw in the human race and favouritism happens whether we like it or not and whether we admit to it or not. I'm sure you'll agree that you would rather work side by side with a wonderful, willing, happy person with few skills than side by side with a nasty, bitter, complaining, negative though skilled professional.

If we are unable to speak up for ourselves or be assertive, we could be ignored and overlooked for promotion, or taken for granted. On the other hand, if we lack technical skills but have a high degree of interpersonal effectiveness, everyone will find it a pleasure to teach us and help us along till we get it right. The company will see us as an asset because a company is a group of people. If a group of people like you a lot, they see you as an asset. Interpersonal skills get you even further than education, training, ability and talent.

In order to form any kind of relationship, we have to interact. We have many different types of relationships - from casual to serious, from shallow to deep and from passing to permanent. If our relationships are solid and positive, we are stable, happy and healthy - physically, mentally and emotionally. If our relationships are negative, we experience many chronic problems in our lives, physically, mentally and emotionally. Negative relationships also lead to practical problems and can be costly too.

Bad relationships with others have the ability to destroy us because the more negativity others treat us with, the more stressed we feel and then we tend to react with negative, reactive, critical, resentful or cynical behaviour in response. They then react in turn to that and it spirals downhill. Why would anyone go out of their way to be nice to me if I am not the kind of person they want to be nice to? People won't want me around if they dislike me. It's as simple as that. And their dislike of me will very likely bring out the worst of me instead of the best of me.

People usually assume that the other is to blame when they have relationship problems. It is, most often, we ourselves who are to blame if we have problems with others. If we learn good, effective interpersonal skills, we will be able to interact with others in such a way that we build and salvage all situations and relationships. The skills, methods and insights necessary to be a much-liked person can be learned and mastered. If you practise and apply them, you will assure yourself of positive, constructive interactions with most people most of the time, through most situations.

Our identity is built out of our relationships with others, for example, we know we are funny if others laugh at our witty comments. We know our insights are interesting if people gather to listen with rapt attention. We know we are liked if people come to the gatherings we host. Our confidence, or lack thereof, has grown out of the rejection or approval we have received from others. The love and acceptance they have given us, or refused to give us, has had a powerful impact on who we have become and where we feel we fit in.

The response we receive from others has the power to shape our destiny. We need our chosen partner to respond to us before he/she can become our lover or spouse. We cannot make friends without the cooperation of those we wish to make friends with. We cannot further our career without the cooperation of others. We cannot be promoted into a senior position without first winning the respect of those above us. We cannot sell goods if we cannot sell ourselves.

In effect there is no such thing as right or wrong because people and their different subjective points of view determine what is either right or wrong for them. Even terrible crimes are often acquitted because the criminal was so likeable that everyone bought into his 'extenuating circumstances'. But what are extenuating circumstances? It is just some clever person able to win the compassion and understanding of a judge or a jury by explaining things using mere words and communication skills. If the criminal is very likeable, the judge and the whole jury simply cannot believe that such a nice person would do such a horrible thing, and they find 'reasonable doubt' in something that wouldn't have worked if the criminal looked and behaved like horrible person. Innocent people have been accused and doomed because they looked and behaved like criminals.

Who knows how much truth is in the words? Right or wrong has got nothing to do with it because people are fallible, influenceable and gullible. If we learn to be effective interpersonally, we can get away with anything, but, if we lack interpersonal skills, we could be doomed. If we feel and behave inferior or suspicious or nervous, we could even come under suspicion and be accused when we are innocent. For all these reasons you can see how vital it is to learn how to get a good response from others.

We do this by first becoming more self-aware and then by becoming more aware of others and the actual results we are getting as we communicate and interact. Become both aware and responsible for the affect you have on others. DO NOT BLAME OTHERS! The minute we blame someone else, we render ourselves utterly helpless. If it is their fault then there is nothing we can do, so we simply have to live with whatever we don't like or want. However, if we take the responsibility, all the responsibility, then there is a whole lot we can do. If you want to win with people you must teach yourself to win, and in order to win, you need to decide to make other people like you, whether they want to or not. No one can make that choice for you but you.

Mirrors

Before we can learn to have excellent relationships with all people, we need to know the half we bring into the equation – ourselves! The best way to find out who we really are is to examine our reactions and responses to others, and theirs to us. We need to examine the effects and results we have in our lives. We need to see how much power or influence people have over us, and vice versa. How many of our choices do we give to others or do we feel are because of others? Who are we in relation to others? When another person meets you, what does he/she see, what does he/she think, how are you perceived by them?

In order to change our lives from survival into an adventure, we need to know who this person is that we are. Once we know who we really are, we can stop trying so hard to be what we think we should be, and clearly see our full potential - what we can become. Once we start progressing towards our full potential, life becomes an exciting, challenging adventure. Every day will have a purpose, we will feel joy, and one day when we are old, we will know we have really lived. The concept of mirrors helps us to see who we are. Once we know who we are, then we know what to change, what to keep and how to influence others positively.

As I've said before, people are only actors on our stage, and all people are our mirrors. Some reflect strongly back at us, some only a weakly. It is the strong mirrors that tell us the most about ourselves - positive and negative. We feel happy, relaxed and comfortable with some people. That is because they are reflecting (mirroring) those parts of ourselves that we are happy, relaxed and comfortable with. Some people bring out negative emotions in us, or we don't like something about them. That is because they are reflecting some part of ourselves, some part of our perceptions, hates or fears that we don't like. Perhaps they trigger negative memories in us.

Whenever we don't like someone, it is seldom the 'person' that we don't like. It is usually the negative mirror that we see in them. The dislike lies in our mind, in the realms of thoughts and ideas on which we base what we choose to like and dislike in people. If we can see the dislike as a mirror to be examined, we can learn something about ourselves. We can look at that part within ourselves, using them as a mirror, and change ourselves. We can also more easily separate the person from the behaviour and look for something else that is likeable about the person instead. Accepting responsibility for our own likes and dislikes, and seeing our judgements of others as useful mirrors, teaches us to look internally and not at the external other. We can then change internally so that we can get along with just about everyone and find peace in the world with all people.

Watch the mirrors! You'll learn so much.

Using mirrors to model others

Let's say you want to learn to feel happy, carefree and relaxed a lot more often. Look around to see in whose company you most easily feel that way? Which people seem to bring you closest or the most often to that space? Now look at them as mirrors reflecting that part of you. Ask yourself some questions. What exactly is it in these people (or person) that makes me feel this way? How can I learn to project this on my own and therefore make myself and others feel this way at will. Copy the good words, behaviours and attitudes of those who generate these states naturally and practise using them. Use others as role models to teach you, and they don't even need to know you're mirroring them and photocopying their great words and behaviours for your use.

Obviously the ability to feel good in the company of particular others exists in yourself somewhere. If they make you feel good it's because you have the ability to feel good. Once you understand more clearly what the person (or people) is reflecting back to you, you will be able to make some distinctions and observations about how you get to feel that way. Their reflecting is illuminating aspects of you. You only need them to bring that out in you until such time as you have learned how to bring it out in yourself, by yourself. The raw ability is in you, and the actual specific skills, mannerisms, behaviours, words and tone of voice are all things you can photocopy for yourself internally and practise.

The same goes for negative mirrors. If someone 'makes' you angry or nervous or uneasy, it is not really they who are making you that way, it is your learned response over time. Now you can single out the people who bring out those

252

feelings in you, and spend a bit of time with them on purpose so you can work out what it is exactly that you don't like, and how you get to feel these negative feelings, and what exactly is so bad about it after all. Work on thinking about why, what and how this happens. You will soon be able to learn what exactly it is about that person that upsets you, and where it exists in your own mind or memories. Then you can find the mirror (or button) in yourself and make the necessary changes so that you begin to really understand yourself.

Eventually you will fully understand all your reactions and emotions. You will have so much more control over your own moods and the states you get into. No matter who is in a bad mood, you will be able to stay happy. No matter who fights with you or becomes difficult, you will be able to keep your peace. No matter how others choose to behave, you'll be able to choose your state regardless. Using mirrors can help you search for and find your own intrinsic happiness. Mirrors help you to search for, find, examine, and then destroy all your buttons and uncomfortable emotions. We can take full responsibility for our own reactions, and therefore our relationships. Once you know who you are, you can then use listening to find out who others are, and silence to get more information about who they really are, and you'll be able to build great relationships with almost anyone.

There never need be any such thing as a personality clash.

Looking at it this way means you can always be delighted to be in anybody's company. Being delighted to be in their company will obviously give them some good reasons and motivation to be delighted in yours. When you like people a

lot, they can't help but like you back. The age-old saying –
love the world and it loves you back! – is true. My wish for
you is that you find a way to get everyone to love you, and a
way to get yourself to love everyone, so you can live a happy
life with everyone in your corner helping you to achieve
your dreams, just because you are such a nice person!

The True School Teachers' Poem

When I am old and review my career,
I want to look back and see memories dear.
I want to know that I did a good job
In the eyes of the children, the rebels, the mob.

That I be remembered for many a year
For never neglecting to wipe every tear.
Ensuring that everyone passing me gained.
That never caused anyone shame or pain.

So many children who could have gone wrong
Instead 'cause of me, are happy and strong.
So many souls I lead by the hour.
So many chances my blessings to shower.

That I'd been a beacon directing the way
For children to follow so no one could stray.
Like flames in the night my integrity burns
And the more love I give, the more love returns.

I want to have answers for all of their trials.
I want to explore many ways, many styles.
I want to have fun every step of the way.
Contented and happy, the end of each day.

What my life becomes is just up to me.
I want to evolve to the best I can be.
I want to be honoured, respected, adored.
I want to have plentiful resources stored.

That I be the teacher that righted the wrongs
And not the subject of cruel playground songs.
That I stand accountable when the bells toll.
All this I ask of myself and my soul

by Terri Ann Laws

Ego

I am going to say 'he' here for ease of writing, but you know of course there are just as many 'she' people in the class I'm about to describe

Here is a man who can only see the world in terms of himself. The world that is happening around him is happening to him and/or because of him. He is unwilling to even listen to or comprehend someone else's point of view. He is driven by both blind instinct and by his own pressing needs, wants and expectations. He learns the *language* of consideration, but the concept escapes him.

He uses the language too. He says, 'You are being selfish,' but he means 'You should sacrifice yourself for me.' He says, 'You are being inconsiderate,' but he means 'Don't consider yourself, consider only me!' He says, 'You are being unfair and greedy,' but he means 'I'm not getting enough. What about me? I want to get more. I want unfairness to be only in my favour!' He uses the language to persuade people that he has the virtue. He talks about fairness, respect and honesty assuming that his use of these words (or his accusing others of lacking these) means that he has these virtues. He does not understand that *something is demanded of him* to be considerate, unselfish and generous, and his own behaviour needs to reflect it.

When he uses the words on other people, he does not always get the good consequences he expects or demands. So he concludes that those who won't pander to him are stupid, blind, wrong or selfish. He is still trying to earn something for himself. All his kindness and good deeds are also designed to earn for himself something in return. He does do kind and good things, but only when he can clearly see that it will benefit himself tenfold. Whenever he gives he thinks he deserves to receive in exchange, and he'll throw any accusations of bad character on people he has given to if they don't give generously in return. The effect he is having on other people does not occur to him, and he won't allow himself to think about it. If anyone is upset with him, it's because they have a problem or they are a problem.

He cannot see other people for who they are, or what they want and need. He can only see them for what their use is to him. He has around him only people who are useful to him and people he can use. He is the centre of the world, and in his world all other people exist only in the capacity of what their existence means for him.

Some people can do things that upset him, so he is careful with them, much in the same way as one is careful of wasps or nettles. Other people wouldn't dare do any things to him, and those people he doesn't worry about. Others he sees as people to get things from, and he collects as many of these as he can. Others he finds he can easily bully, use or manipulate to do things for him that he rightly should do for himself, and he hangs on to a few of those people too. Those that he has no use for, and those who are no threat to him, are completely ignores.

Everything is given a value or a place in his life in terms of himself and the effects or consequences to himself only. Self and self-gain are his only consciousness and goal and he sees nothing else. He can be charming, entertaining or delightful at times because he has learned that this is the greatest human fishing rod and bait. He does not see the larger picture, he does not see life in general, he does not see other people as separate human beings with their own different likes, wants and needs. He only sees himself. We call this total self 'ego-bound' or narcissistic.

Somewhere between this total extreme and the opposite extreme (people who live their lives entirely and only for others at expense to themselves), lie the bulk of the population. Sadly, too many adults in our world exist further along the ego side of the continuum than along the selfless side of it. The best place to be is balanced right in the middle, able to take care of ourselves and equally able to take care of others.

Some people never mature very far past this barrier of ego. The great 'I am' blinds them to the effects they may have on others. This renders them unable to see life from someone else's point of view, and make the best decisions for the long-term good of all. The immediate gratification of self is all they can see. They feel strong, hostile emotions if anyone dares find any fault with them. Some of them display these emotions, others brood on them internally and become silently spiteful. Yet these ego-bound people happily find fault with anyone and everyone else. Like children, they depend on praise - in fact they often demand praise - but they only dish out praise to people who pander to them or feed their ego. Unless they have personally gained from someone else's goodness, they will not recognise the goodness or the person.

Once we have grown up and accepted full responsibility for ourselves, our own happiness, our circumstances and - most importantly - for the effects we have on others, we become more free of ego. We can still be child like, playful, selfish, authoritarian or anything else we choose, but we no longer feel compelled to react in certain ways in order to survive. We no longer feel compelled to manipulate others. Once we have an intrinsic sense of our own value, our own worth in the greater scheme of things, we can concentrate on the purpose and not the pay-off.

It sounds illogical and paradoxical, but the more value we place on ourselves, the less we are controlled by ego. The more we value ourselves as good people, the more concerned we become for others and the value they place on themselves. The less approval we need, the more approval we are able to give. The bigger and more whole and more capable we see ourselves, the safer we try to make others feel. The bigger we actually are, the less we need to prove and the less we need to use others.

Definition of ego

- Wanting them to see your point of view - but you don't want to see theirs.
- Wanting them to be nice to you - but you don't want to be nice to them.
- Wanting them to put you first - but you don't want to put them first.
- Wanting everyone to say nice things about you - but you don't want to say nice things about them.
- Wanting them to understand you, but you don't want to understand them.
- Wanting them to be guilty and/or in the wrong - but you don't want to be guilty or in the wrong.
- Wanting them to say sorry to you - but you don't want to say sorry to them.
- Wanting them to trust you, but you don't want to trust them.
- Wanting them to give you credit - but you don't want to give them credit.
- Wanting them to believe you - but you don't want to believe them.
- Finding faults in them, but insisting that you do not have any of those faults yourself.
- Being convinced that you are right and they are wrong, unwilling to investigate their point of view to see why they are also right.

An ego-bound individual is a nightmare to everyone who knows them, including themselves, because they are in so much hurt and pain and feel so much fury every time the world will not devote itself to making them happy. They live a narrow, shallow existence plagued by negative thoughts and are surrounded by the people they control, dominate, manipulate and use. The joy they experience is always fleeting and the agony, depression and frustration they experience is vast. Very often they are on medication or they drink too much or suffer some kind of chronic condition. They are not free, they are trapped and often they are also bitter, resentful or depressed.

Buddhists believe that ego is the main cause of human pain and suffering. They could be right. We all have a bit of ego in us, some more than others. Fully conquering the ego is a massive achievement and definitely results in finding far greater peace, happiness and inner joy in life. You can then make others happy and then they'll make you happy because they want to, not because they are manipulated or scared of you.

Know you are very valuable just as you are, therefore you have nothing to prove, and there is no one who needs to be brought down a peg or two, since they aren't above you. No one is above you and no one is beneath you. Your mission in life is to improve yourself only, nobody else. Help others see that they are valuable too. Don't expect others to be an advocate, protector or provider for you. Rather be that way for yourself. Start taking full responsibility for your feelings. Start taking full responsibility for your expectations. Never accuse anyone of a fault unless you too have that fault. Be a nurturer not a demander. Be a leader not a bully. Be part of the solution, not part of the problem. Approve of others and help them feel safe. Love yourself and love others and always look at the bigger picture and be willing to put yourself in the shoes of others and imagine what they might be going through.

Conquering the ego in us takes us leaps and bounds towards a life of peace, joy, happiness and love with strong meaningful relationships. If the Buddha is correct (and I suspect he is) then conquering your ego will result in you being in a delightful state of bliss all the time, everyone will love you, no one will feel threatened by you, you'll have no enemies only friends and you will go happily and joyfully through life making all your dreams come true with ease.

Behaviour Changer

Because we are creatures of habit, most of us find it very difficult to stop behaving in a way we don't like. We find it just as difficult to start doing the things we keep putting off, or don't know how to do. Change can sometimes be difficult only because habits are so deep and automatic, so spontaneous and unconscious. The good news is that good practice and good habits stick just as surely, once we get them into our body and neurology, and it is just as difficult to break a good habit. Once we've broken a bad habit and installed something good in its place, the new thing runs on automatic unconsciously without effort in place of the old thing, all by itself and becomes the new habit. All behaviours habituate.

The big struggle is not such a struggle anymore because new human technologies have found us easy ways to change habits and install new ones. The only effort is doing the processes. If it is done properly in the first place, it happens quite quickly.

Installing new behaviour

When you catch yourself doing something you no longer want to do, say to yourself, 'Thank you for pointing that out to me.' Then run a fantasy movie in your head of yourself doing it the way you should have done it, or want to do it in future. Run the movie from the beginning to the end several times in your mind, and be sure to feel good while you're doing it. Put a smile on your face and enjoy doing it the right way in your mind. This way you have some practice doing the right thing in the right way. With bio-feedback technology, scientists have discovered that our bodies respond as strongly and in the same way to things we imagine as it does to things we actually do or experience. Your brain cannot tell the difference between what is real and what is vividly imagined, so the practice you get this way will be real practice and will work just as well as if you had physically done it.

After a few times you will find you catch yourself physically in the act of playing out your old pattern or habit. That is the moment when permanent change begins. You break the habit or pattern in mid swing and immediately begin doing the new thing instead.

When my kids were small, they discovered it was relatively easy to get me to say yes after I'd said no if they just put up a big enough fuss. It didn't always work, but sometimes they would go to great lengths, and when I was determined not to change my mind for my good reasons, they would lay it on very thick until I lost it and yelled at them. I didn't want to yell at them anymore and realised I needed a new habit. So, after each time I forgot and yelled, I thanked myself for noticing. I imagined myself calmly explaining to my kids that no amount of pleading from them was going to make me change my mind because my answer was 'no'.

I pictured them making their usual performance and still I calmly said 'no', remaining loving, relaxed and aloof and impervious to any antics or manipulations from them. I kept running the movie, seeing myself calm and relaxed and composed regardless of what they were doing or saying, and in my mind I kept saying 'no' until I imagined the kids realising it was pointless bothering me. I pictured the kids taking 'no' for an answer. I ran the movie often from start to finish.

A few days later I caught myself starting to yell. I stopped in mid-sentence. Immediately I took a deep breath. The kids stared at me waiting for it. I held my breath for a few seconds and then calmly said, 'No.' I got the usual objections, and still I calmly said 'no'. They tried harder and harder but I kept my cool and repeated, 'No.' Eventually they got fed up and bored and went away. The old pattern was broken and the new one was firmly in place and I never needed to yell at my kids again because they realised they could no longer bully me into saying 'yes'.

This 'movie' method is particularly useful when it comes to learning to behave in a way you've never behaved before and cannot get a chance to practise. This can be used for doing anything new, like going to an interview and practising being your best at it. You can use it to install great skills you never thought you'd have. People have used it to install things like leadership qualities, management ability, and the confidence to speak in public. To learn something totally new to you, find a person who does the thing very well naturally, and then watch them closely. Take in every little detail of their behaviour including their stance, gestures, tone of voice, eye contact, expressions, everything. You can watch them many times and practise being like that yourself. You'll be surprised how quickly you get it into your body and mind. Kids learn almost everything by imagining in this way.

There are other wonderful ways to install new behaviours into your body and automatic nervous system, and the movie way is one way, the tape recorder or Dictaphone way is another. You'll need a Dictaphone or a tape deck and then to do this.

1. Write a letter to yourself starting with 'I used to ... (describe the unwanted behaviour, habit or pattern). But then I realised that it was causing ... (describe the symptoms, consequences, whatever, that are unwanted). So now instead I ... (describe the new behaviour, habit etc. that you intend to do instead). And since I have been doing this, I find ... (describe the wanted good consequences, results and effects).

2. Then read this letter on to your Dictaphone or tape. Play it for yourself first thing in the morning as you open your eyes, before you get up. Play it again last thing at night as you're falling asleep. This is a wonderful way to 'talk' to your subconscious or semi-conscious mind. It goes in deeply when you're half asleep.

3. Then, for your conscious mind, set goals and write out some affirmations and stick them on the fridge. The words could be something like, 'I am so happy and grateful now that I ... (fill in the new behaviour)' You could also list all the good qualities, habits or

behaviours on a piece of paper in point form. Get yourself a 'goal bowl' (I have a pretty glass bowl next to my bed) and put the list in it. Read it a few times during the day, telling your brain and higher conscious to pay attention and remind you at the moment when you need it. Put a similar kind of bowl on your desk at work and keep your paperclips or something in it. This bowl can be empty if you like, and will serve only to remind you of your goal bowl at home.

4. Set a time frame for when you want to be perfect at the new behaviour. At the end of your goals list write: 'I can already do this and I prove it more every day. The more I practise and remember, the better and better I get.'

Some people promise themselves they'll do this but then never get around to actually doing it. Anthony Robbins has a marvellous way of getting us to make ourselves take action (Personal Power 11). He calls it 'The Dickens Pattern'. He says if you think of all the things you miss out on, all the things you can't have and can't do, all the ways in which you suffer or struggle, then you'll want to do it more. Imagine the problem growing worse every year until it is totally unbearable. You'll want to escape the pain of not changing if you elaborate on the pain and negative consequences and scare yourself into taking action now. Follow this up by imagining how fantastic it will be when you've made the change.

If the desire to do it is strong enough, you'll do it. So work on increasing your desire. The next thing to do is to think of all the things you'll gain, all the ways in which your life will be much better, all the benefits and bonuses you'll get when you've done it, so you also increase your desire to do it. The stronger the desire, the easier it is to get yourself to take action on it.

Daydream a lot, but always daydream about yourself in successful positions and wonderful circumstances. Never daydream about what can or has gone wrong. When you are going to sleep at night, fill your mind with wonderful, happy thoughts. Picture yourself doing all the things you want to do and becoming the kind of person you want to be. We usually dream about the last thing that was on our mind as we fell asleep. So this practice will give you lots of good dreams. The more you do this, the more you'll be able to see yourself really doing and having what you want, and the less doubts you'll have.

Have fun and enjoy building your dreams and installing all the great behaviours you want.

Worry and Fear

When the worst that can happen actually happens, we find ourselves stronger than ever. We do not suffer as terribly, or fall apart and die, as we imagined we would.

An old lady stood in her nightgown on the pavement at 2 a.m. one morning, staring in stunned disbelief as mighty flames tore into the heavens, separating her entire life into ashes and smoke. She began to shiver as she thought of her warm bed, tea, slippers and heater. She shivered worse when she thought of all her expensive and priceless belongings that she had devoted her entire life to collecting. What else had she done with her life? Nothing! She had spent it collecting all the things that were now roaring into oblivion.

Next morning in hospital, all her friends and family came to her bedside to comfort her. Expecting to find her in a terrible state of tears, shock and fear over her loss, they were surprised to find her in the best of spirits, laughing and talking loudly with great excitement - a thing she had never done as long as they'd known her. 'She has lost her mind,' someone whispered.

But she had not lost her mind. On the contrary, she had found it. "I'm free!" she exclaimed. "I was trapped in my own prison of precious, priceless belongings. I was afraid to leave the house in case someone broke in, I was afraid to have people over in case they stole, spoiled or broke something, I was suspicious of my children, and afraid they were waiting for me to die so they could inherit my things. I see it all now. I was wasting my life! My belongings made me bitter, nasty, clinging, fearful and unfriendly. They made me suspicious and kept me from getting close to my loved ones. Now I feel wonderful; I feel so free."

I was watching on TV one day, an endless stream of refugees walking in search of a new home and country. I thought to myself. 'What an amazing experience! What a deep, intense, incredible experience! I wonder what that must feel like?' Can you imagine being part of something like that? Having absolutely nothing to lose and all together in the same situation!

Your life is a movie. It isn't real even though it seems very real. If you've read everything in this book so far, you might have become aware of a great secret that great people have always known, but the general population have been unaware of. The great secret is that whatever you focus your attention on, think about all the time and feel strongly about, shows up in your life in one form or another over and over again. Whatever you believe you are right, and life will prove you right. If you have a lot of fears and worries and you spend a lot of time feeling fearful and worrying, life will throw some things at you to give you reasons to carry on feeling fearful and worrying, because life will prove you right whatever you believe without a doubt in your deepest being.

Spending thought, time, energy and emotion on worry and fear has the sad consequence of attracting unfortunate happenings into your life; bad luck increases and many things go wrong. Feeling helpless will make you helpless. These kinds of thoughts and feelings also cause premature ageing, stress and deplete your immune system, eventually eroding your health and body resilience. Medical science has now proved that up to 90% of all disease, chronic and acute, is essentially the result of stress. People who are happy, positive, enjoying life and feeling optimistic, very seldom get sick. In fact even when there is genetic disease in the family, such as arthritis or diabetes, very few of the happy, positive family members get the disease. Medical science is at last paying more attention to these facts and a lot more research is going into the phenomenon. Only about 1% of the happy, optimistic, positive family members get the family's genetic diseases and conditions, while often as much as 30% (some studies say this number is much higher) of the stressed, unhappy, sad, worried, negative or inactive family members get them.

Living a joy-filled life of trust and positive expectancy is a much happier, richer life and actually has the result of creating more good luck, more fortunate coincidences, better physical health and better life conditions. If you look at it logically, you can see that a person feeling fearful and worried is less likely to go out and make things happen. A person feeling hopeful and safe and positive is more likely to go out and do things, achieve things, change things and make things happen. The more a person does things and makes things happen, the more skills they acquire, the more people they get to know, the more resourcefulness they learn and the more they become capable of changing things they don't want. They are also fitter, healthier and more resilient. The happier and safer you feel in the world, the more willing and able you are to go out and make life safe and prosperous for yourself.

If you believe the world is wonderful safe place full of opportunities, excitement, great people and amazing experiences, you are right. If you believe the world is a dangerous place full of crime, violence and the constant threat of war and terrorist attacks you are also right. There are people everywhere who believe one or the other their whole lives long, and the quality of their lives reflects what they believe. Both can be seen as true, it depends where you look and what you focus on. You can spend your time reading the holiday and 'great getaway breaks' part of the newspaper, or you can read all the gory bits about war, murder and treachery. The way you feel all day after that, the way you feel about life and the way you live your life will reflect where you are putting your attention.

It is possible for anyone to accept the fact that there are dangers in the world and everyone eventually dies, and then forget about all that totally. Thinking and fearing and worrying about it are not going to help in any way. Rather spend every waking minute of your days thinking about and focusing on all the fun, happy, good things there are to do and achieve and enjoy. Expect the best and dream of having the best and then you'll have many hours of joy in every day. If things do go wrong at some point, or if something terrible does happen, there will be time enough to deal with it then. There is no point giving it one moment of your time or attention in advance, since it might never happen anyway. Certainly you don't want to be wasting precious 'happy' time giving thought to things you don't want or don't like and feeling awful for nothing. Feel good. Feeling good is a choice and it affords you a fantastic quality of life all of every day.

If you feel sick with fear and worry, remember:
- The worst that can happen could be challenging, exciting and fascinating.
- If you fear death, you probably fear life more.
- You **are** going to die. You have no choice, you have no escape, you are definitely going to die, so forget it. It is the only guarantee that comes with birth. It is the most reliable fact on Earth. Best you start living with all your heart while you are still alive, and never waste a single day.
- If you fear your loved ones dying, remember that they do not belong to you. They belong to the universe and nature. It is not your place to decide if, how or when they should die. There is nothing you can do about it, so **let go**. They are definitely going to die some day, and it is not up to you how or when, so enjoy them and let go.
- If you are going to be a fool, be a fool on purpose. Be the very best fool you can be.
- Whatever terrible thing could happen, it would be great to have the experience so that you can learn something new, how to make the most of it, how to use it to your advantage or turn it into a brag story.

Then that thing can never hold you hostage or ransom or scare you again.

- Life is a daily journey, not a destination. The more you experience, the more memories you collect, the more you have to talk about, the bigger your horizons expand.

- Most fears are in the imagination and have no basis in fact. Once confronted, they usually vanish. The acronym FEAR stands for False Evidence that Appears Real.

- A coward dies a thousand deaths, a courageous man only one. Every time we imagine the worst we experience it in our minds and live through the whole terrible experience for nothing.

- In order to sail in search of new lands, one has to be willing to lose sight of the shore. Be willing to lose sight of the shore.

- Excitement, adventure and discovery are far more enriching and rewarding than security, safety and monotony.

- If you are afraid of doing it badly, your fear will work against you and cause you to lose confidence and do badly. Be willing to do it badly. What's more important anyway - others opinions or your experience?

- If every one of us is different, then each of us is unique. If something is unique, it is the only existing sample of itself. It must therefore be perfect. Be yourself.

- If you try to be different from what you are, or if you try to be like someone else, you are trying to be imperfect. That is also fine, but give yourself time to learn and practise until you can be someone else well.

- The very worst that can happen is nothing. If nothing happens, your life is empty, meaningless and boring.
- Worry is a bad habit and the more you practise it, the better you get at it. Start practising something else instead.
- Lions kill buck, even buck with babies. Bees sting and bogs bite. Get with the program and take life as it comes and deal only with the problems that actually confront you, not with the problems that MIGHT confront you.
- Let go and let God. Being God is a huge task, so rather let Him/Her do it. Enjoy the moment and only entertain good, happy, positive thoughts.
- Stop all worry because you worrying won't change a thing except the speed at which you age. Worry causes premature ageing!!!!

Have fun in life, think only of good things and worry no more

States of Bliss

I have the gift of blissful states; I use it all the time.
Whenever trouble comes my way I use these states of mine.

When the world goes cruel and mad, how scary things can
seem.
I take a breath, call my states, raise my eyes and dream.

Pain and fear and heartache - have little hold on me.
I feel them, then I quickly choose a state to set me free.

When worries sneaks up on me and feel panic in my chest,
I quickly call a better state and let it do the rest.

I would get hurt, at times I'd cry and sometimes felt alone.
I would get angry, jealous, scared and miserable and moan.

But oh I hated all those times of feeling so much pain.
That's why I learned my special gift and wiped away the
stain.

I didn't always have this gift, I found it there one day,
And had to study very hard to use it the right way.

Sometimes it confuses some new people that I meet
When they see me smiling when I should be shocked as sheet

But that's because they foolishly believe themselves to be
The helpless victims of events and things they hear and see

They feel obliged to hurt and cry and lose control and break
They think it's wrong to rise above, convinced it must be
fake

The loss is clearly theirs I fear, they know not what they miss
For I can dance with angels and enjoy my states of bliss.

by Terri Ann Laws

Help I'm Going Crazy!

Here is a bit of good advice to help you make the changes you want to make quickly and to help the changes stick.

1. Share everything you learn with at least one person within a day or two - before you forget it. Sharing helps you remember it. People may disagree with you or ask for clarity. This is excellent because it helps you think more deeply about it. It calls upon you to look for examples and learn it better. Unless the information becomes real to you and stays with you, it will become lost and forgotten. Make notes and write affirmations. See how things apply to your own life so that you learn for the first person singular - you.

2. Do not stop reading, learning, assimilating, applying, practising and growing until you have grown much bigger than all the problems you face. If you do not actually use and apply the information you gather, and practically experience it, you may become well informed, but not free, not healed, and not happy. Albert Einstein said, 'We can't solve our problems at the level of thinking that created them.'

3. Learn how to value, honour, trust, appreciate, know and love yourself. You are your own mentor, teacher, parent, child, instructor, friend and guide. The child the teacher is always picking on never improves, and in fact gets worse. The child the teacher encourages and is proud of, does better and better. You are your own child and teacher. You are your most important asset. Take very good care of yourself.

4. If you can do building alterations to your house and improvements and repairs to your car, why can't you do that to yourself? You can buy a new house or car, but you cannot buy a new body or mind - so look after, repair, restore, improve and update yourself. Nurture, treasure, maintain and love yourself. You are absolutely precious and priceless - especially to yourself.

5. Take full responsibility for your life. It is your life and no one else can live it for you. It is no one else's job to make you happy. No one else is obliged to sacrifice their life for your happiness or convenience. You can do this for yourself, and you'll find that you are more reliable than anyone else when it comes to taking care of you.

6. Take full responsibility for the effect you have on others. It is up to you to earn or to learn how to get the response you want. Look for and find what you are doing 'wrong' so that you can put it right. If you don't correct the things that you are doing wrong in your life, then the things that are going wrong will continue to happen. Self-righteousness, denial, justifications and blame- throwing keep people stuck! We create our own reality and our own destiny.

7. In order for things to go wrong in our lives, we have to be doing a few things 'wrong' (ineffective) to cause it. If other people have things they should change (own up to, apologize for, stop doing or start doing) then so must we too. Until we are willing to be wrong, we can never come right. Guilt (or regret) is feeling you have done something wrong - freedom is knowing it and fixing it! Guilt is suffering under

280

the feeling, looking desperately for escape, wanting with all your heart to be proved innocent - freedom is being grateful you can feel it so that you are forced, prompted and motivated to search for it, find it, and fix it. Guilt is natural. It is a friend not an enemy. It is a loud warning bell that cannot be silenced by drugs, rationalization or encouragement, because these are all attempts at denial. Freedom begins with self- honesty, a reality check and a good mental and emotional clean out.

8. Do not allow yourself to be or feel alienated. Alienation is a scary, lonely place. Become one with the world, one with yourself, one with your loved ones, and one with mankind. Feel part of the planet, the animal kingdom, the plants and flowers. Look at the trees, the birds, the mountains and the sea. They are all yours and you are theirs. Feel a deep sense of belonging and connection. Lie outside at night and stare at the stars, or sit on a rock in the sunlight and stare at the trees. They are all yours and you are theirs. Float among the clouds. You are safe and welcome. Every little butterfly is special, and so are you.

9. Do not separate yourself from the human race by finding fault or feeling worth less or superior or inferior or different from others. Everything you do or say affects others, just as they affect you. We are all connected like drops of water in the river, flowing, rushing, falling and spreading together on this journey of life from the source to the sea. Connect up and enjoy the ride. You are never alone, no matter how alone you may sometimes feel. Find

out who you really are! It is the most fantastic journey.

I'll let you in on another little secret - once we are really willing to be wrong, completely wrong, we discover that there is no such thing as wrong. It is the most fantastic and amazing thing. We actually completely stop accusing ourselves and others - not as a result of some noble choice, but because something inside really changes and finds a different space to exist in. It's only through understanding, owning and admitting to 'wrong' that we can dismantle it and shed it forever. Wrong only means that there is a better choice out there, that will feel better and create better results.

I caught my breath to see that I was breathing,
I opened up my soul to vultures feeding,
And then I was surprised when I was bleeding,
And always, I'm reaching out to me.

I spoke too many words and they were streaming,
I couldn't seem to harness all my dreaming,
I thought I was at peace but I was screaming,
And always, I'm reaching out to me.

They laughed at me, I didn't like the feeling,
I couldn't seem to dis-encode their meaning,
Did my garden really need such weeding?
And always, I'm reaching out to me.

The prophets spoke the wisdom I was heeding,
They seemed to give me everything I was needing,
Until I realized it's me I'm seeding,
And always, I'm reaching out to me,

Searching for my freedom,
when all the time I'm free.

by Terri Ann Laws

Poems

'What are all the poems about?', You might say. Well, I've coached, counselled and helped so many thousands of people over many years and got them to really enjoy life and follow their dreams. I write humorous poems now and then to tease people (lovingly of course) when they have got stuck in some negative thinking or negative life pattern. Some of them you've already encountered in the book. I wrote this following poem for a very depressed woman, and it was so apt, so terribly true, that she burst out laughing and said, 'I get your point,' and she immediately began to change her life around completely.

Leave me to sleep off my hours,
my dreams are more pleasant than life.
Leave me alone with my tablets,
they combat my worry and strife.

Don't frighten me with the future,
you know I don't want to go on,
Endlessly slogging and climbing,
so pointless and endless and long.

Life is a desperate struggle.
There's really no point to it all.
I cannot imagine the future.
I know if I try I will fall.

I only beg that you pardon,
what you interpret as sin,
me lying under my duvet
while you say I mustn't give in.

by Terri Ann Laws

She admitted she was wallowing in self-pity and was in some peculiar way proud of the fact that her life had been the hardest, cruellest, most difficult life anyone had ever lived. But she hadn't realized what a terrible burden she had been placing on her loved ones and family, and how she had expected them to honour her suffering rather than honour the hopes and dreams they had for themselves. She realised that she was making her loved ones pay for the suffering she had, and in so doing, she was doing exactly the same to them that was done to her, she was perpetuating the problem into the next generation.

Coping Skills

The following may help you when you feel:

Guilt: Ask yourself some serious questions. Is this my induced conscience or my natural conscience? Is this guilt really mine? Have I in fact done something wrong? If you have, do not justify it - admit it. Make amends if you possibly can. Have courage, compassion, empathy and power. Fix it as soon as possible. It does us far better to take the blame than to avoid it, because we can do something about a problem that is ours. If the guilt is not yours, then drop it.

Fear: First of all, recognize it and admit it. Say it aloud if you can. Shout out loud, 'I feel fear!' Then notice where in your body you feel it. Put your hand on that place and be curious about how you feel fear. Then breathe deeply and breathe all the fear out. Think - what is the worst that can possibly happen? Is that really so bad? Is it worse than now? Wouldn't it be fascinating to see what happens, and learn a whole lot in the process? See what you are capable of. You might surprise yourself. Most fears disappear once confronted, because most are in the imagination. Fear is an energy, use the energy constructively. Remember: F.E.A.R = False Evidence that Appears Real.

Anger: Anger is better than apathy, depression or despondency. Admit your anger and if possible, confess it out loud. Shout out loud, 'I feel anger!' Then notice where in your body you feel it. Put your hand on that place and be curious about how you do anger. Then breathe deeply and breathe all the anger out. Another choice is to rip up an old telephone directory or something until you're laughing. It is far better to say you are angry than to behave in an angry way (like hitting someone or yelling). If the anger is very intense, release some of it in a safe way in a safe place (bury your head in a pillow and scream). Use your anger to motivate you into action. Anger is power energy! Don't waste it - channel it and use it to do something constructive. See it as a roaring waterfall that could be used to move things along and generate electricity at the same time. Change anger into motivation

Depression:. Take one moment at a time. Live in the short run and not in the long run. Ignore logic if it tells you nothing can be done. Detach. Do something, create something or visit somebody. Do a kind deed and do not get found out. Give just a little time, love or energy away. Phone a friend to cheer yourself up. Decide to stop choosing your depressed response. Ask yourself, 'What needs to happen for me to feel depressed?' Notice how it starts, and then you'll recognize it in time to quickly do something else to take your mind away from the feeling. Decide what you'll feel instead from now on, and then practise it, using the new behaviour method. Whatever you practise you get good at. The more you practise depression, the better you get at it. Use the Behaviour Changer. Practise feeling happy and motivated and energized, and soon you will master it. Nothing is easy at first, but all things become easy with practice.

Overload:. Take one step at a time. Do one thing at a time, and do not stop doing it until you have finished. Prioritize all the things you have to do on paper. Do them one by one to the best of your ability, without allowing any interruptions. Tick them off as you finish them. Stay focused and work systematically. Remove all the distractions you possibly can that would take you away from your purpose, for example, turn off the telephone. Give yourself time. Leave your watch in another room if you can. If you have too many things to do in one day, ask someone to help you or delegate. Take five minutes and clear your mind and think of a calm river or a beautiful scene in nature. Breathe deeply and relax. Then get on with systematically going through the things you need to do, keeping that calm feeling with you.

Worry:. Mind your own business. You cannot play God. You will never have control over other people, fate, circumstances, accidents, the world's affairs or anything else. Worry is only the imagination creating a mental image of the worst that can happen. Stop it, let go and practise the art of allowing. Worry is also energy. Use the energy positively and make yourself busy with it. Worry is using your imagination destructively. Rather use your imagination constructively and imagine the best that can happen.

Obsessive thinking:. When you simply can't stop thinking about something and the thoughts are turning round and round in your mind, driving you crazy – meditate or go for a run with headphones on, listening to some inspirational speaker or an interesting story. Learn to clear your mind. You can learn to relax your mind by focusing on relaxing your body. Sit or lie down comfortably. Think about your toes: toe nails, bones, skin. Then move on to your feet: arches, bones, skin, heel. Then your ankles, then your calves, ... and on you go up through your whole body, one bit at a time, right up to your hair. Eventually you will learn to think what you choose to think. Your mind is your servant, not your master. You are not your mind, you have a mind, and you know that because you can change your mind. Alternatively, take yourself on a fantasy imagination trip to the most exciting place you can think of to go, or even take a fantasy trip through fairyland. Get control of your mind. It is easier than you might imagine.

Another little list of coping tools

1. The art of diplomacy. Learn the art of saying even the most offensive thing in the most inoffensive way. This will help to at least get a hearing. It will help you talk to people about sensitive issues without starting an argument or causing resentment. It will help you to get your own way and have others happy to give it to you. We always make allowances and give more to people who are so polite and nice. Without diplomacy we might find ourselves upsetting people even though we have the best intentions. Notice who you're speaking to and take that into account, and speak on their terms with courage and consideration, being as nice, polite, friendly and diplomatic as you

can, but hold your head high and feel strong as you do it.

2. One moment at a time. When you feel you are not coping, emotionally, mentally or physically, take it one moment at a time. Forget about yesterday, forget about tomorrow, forget about the consequences. As long as you are doing the best you can with the best intentions for the long-term good of everyone concerned, that's all that is ever expected of you. At any given moment in time, you only have to cope with that one moment.

3. Detachment. When things are getting too much for you, or people around you are reacting like mad, or everything has gone wrong, and there is nothing you can do, just detach. Remove yourself mentally and emotionally from the scene and watch (both them and yourself) as though you were a fly on the wall. This helps you to see the whole thing objectively, and get a grip. Remove yourself mentally and disconnect from it. It helps you to be able to choose your feelings and responses. It helps to not be emotionally or adversely affected by what is going on around you.

4. Visualization. Train yourself mentally by using your imagination. You can dream in the perfect life for yourself and then you'll begin to get good ideas of how to make it happen. Visualize the perfect outcome before doing things that are new or difficult so that when you find yourself in the real situation, it isn't totally new to you, and you've practised in the best response. The more vivid and real you imagine it the better. Add all the senses, visual, auditory,

feeling, touch, taste and smell. You can practise new habits, new approaches and new responses this way. You can dream up better ways of handling things as long as you always visualize the best possible alternatives and the happiest endings. Life becomes what you imagine it to be, and there is no better way to create your own reality than by making it happen using rich, detailed visualizations.

5. Affirmation. Keep little cards with you or stick up notes for yourself in places where you will see them often to remind yourself of something. For example: 'Remember to practise more patience.' Or 'Allow them and let go', or 'Have courage and consideration!' These affirmations serve to help you change habits or patterns. They also help to keep you focused when you're trying to learn a new skill. They remind you all the time of what you want to be focusing on.

6. Mirrors. Remember, we can only see in others, things that are present somewhere in ourselves. If we want to know how we are progressing, or what we need to work on, we only have to watch the mirrors all around us. Allow all people to be your mirrors. Then when you look at them, don't see only them – see reflections of parts of yourself as well. Using people are mirrors helps you discover what in you needs changing or updating, it helps you to separate the person from the problem and it also helps you with investigating human beings in general so you can pick the best qualities to re-make yourself how you really want to be. Seeing people as mirrors affords you the gift of replacing frustration and annoyance

you might feel with compassion and understanding instead.

7. Outcomes. Always decide what you DO want (not what you don't want) and describe it in lots of detail. This way you know what to move towards instead of only knowing what to avoid. If you spend your life heading for a dream, life is exciting and motivating and challenging. If you spend your life avoiding what you don't want, you're remembering all the bad things and dangers all the time. This can get you feeling depressed, de-motivated or overwhelmed. You already know what you don't want, so forget about it and focus only on what you do want. Then only focus forwards on getting what you do want, and do not focus on avoiding what you don't want. Keep the end in mind; the positive end result that you want.

8. Mental movies. Make sure all the movies you run in your head are happy, inspiring memories, fun things, people and places you love and especially dreams of the future. See yourself as a great hero enjoying all the things you want in life and being the kind of person you want to be. Retire away all your old, misery movies that make you feel negative or bad in any way. You've run them enough times; you've felt bad enough times already, so throw them out. Going through all that horrible stuff, feeling all that pain was bad enough at the time. There is absolutely no point in torturing yourself by reviewing the movie and reliving all that old pain again. Revive all the fabulous memories and movies from the past and

run those instead, and run lots of great dream movies too.

Integrity

You will be surprised how many people don't have a clue what integrity is. They simply cannot see the difference between what is constructive and good for mankind and what is destructive and likely to produce lots of negative consequences. They have very self-gaining ideas about right and wrong, good and bad, healthy, constructive behaviour and unhealthy, destructive behaviour. This is because society has forced us through punishment and reward, rejection and praise all our lives to 'please' adults and others against our better judgement. We've been told from small to put others first, but we've actually experienced everyone putting themselves first, and we've not experienced people putting us first. It is all so incongruent and wacky that no one really knows how to put others first and still survive and get the best deal for themselves.

All our lives we've been taught to be fake in the name of politeness, self-sacrifice, consideration, fairness etc., and no one is really looking out for the best interests of others. All these supposedly 'good' and 'unselfish' things are forced on a child who cannot comprehend the reasons why, or who has very good reasons for not wanting to comply. As a result, we learn to be false, to feel cheated, to tell white lies and to have hidden agendas. Society doesn't match up to what it preaches, and all of us are stuck in the middle of this duality doing the best we can to survive, while also doing the best we can to be good people, and the two conflict constantly. It is no wonder that most people haven't got a clue what integrity actually is!

When it comes to the lifeboat scenario, you have to save yourself first because unless you are safe and sound in the lifeboat, you can't rescue others or you'll both drown and they'll blame you. You are the most important person on the planet. Having integrity is right and you will find it does work for you. It builds long term, reliable bonds of friendship, trust and permanence, and you seldom have to sacrifice yourself for others, because with right thinking and common sense and a clear understanding of true integrity, you can always negotiate a fair win/win every time. It will only be in the very rare exceptional occasion that you might have to choose to forgo integrity in order to save yourself (or save someone dear to you).

In order to prevent judgement, guilt or feelings of inadequacy from creeping in, it is better to see integrity as a goal to strive towards rather than a state you 'should' be in, or virtues you 'ought' to possess. Having integrity makes a person a very easy to trust and very likeable so you are glad to know them and will always recommend them as a great character. Having integrity gives you power and ensures you will always have a clean conscience; a clean reputation and you'll always feel good about yourself. If all of us learn to recognise what integrity actually is, then not only can we hold ourselves to it, but we can insist that others operate with integrity too. We can collectively refuse to allow others to operate with a lack of integrity and then we can make the world a much better, fairer and safer place for all. We need to be operating from the same set of rules collectively, then we'll have no victims and villains, no rip-off and con artists and we can do dealings with each other that enrich everyone.

I believe in this dream in spite of the comments of the cynics and naysayers. I truly believe we can create a world where everyone lives in integrity.

It is hard to describe integrity. Perhaps the best way to begin is to say what it isn't. Integrity is NOT:

1. Twisting the truth and believing the new version yourself.

2. Allowing pride or ego or self-righteousness to dictate what choices you make.

3. Justifying yourself.

4. Refusing to accept responsibility for your words or actions, assuming circumstances excuse you.

5. Looking out for number one (yourself and your own) regardless of the consequences to others.

6. Using people and/or taking advantage of people.

7. Telling lies.

8. Distrusting people. Being suspicious. (This is actually a symptom of lack of integrity.)

9. Forcing, tricking, frightening or manipulating people into doing what you want

10. Being dishonest about your real intentions, reasons or actions. (having a secret plot or secret motive).

11. Having excellent reasons why you are always forced to break your promises or your word.

12. Avoiding confrontation at all costs or when it is unavoidable, using tactics to get your own way.

13. Creating or inventing reasons why the other person is wrong or bad to justify ripping them off, taking what's not yours or leaving them out in the cold.

14. Allowing greed or jealousy to rob your common sense, decency or consideration. For example, it is frightening how many people discover pure evil in their closest friends and family members after winning the lottery or coming into money some other way. Treachery, trickery, lies, deceit and even murder is not uncommon when greed and jealousy enter the stage, and the winners (or earners) of money have discovered the heart-breaking truth of the nature of the human race – especially when it surfaces in their nearest and dearest.

15. Being unwilling to look at all things from all perspectives and to see things from the other person's point of view and consider the consequences to others.

16. Telling everyone and getting lots of people in your corner by telling them your version of the story when you have a problem or negative encounter with someone, and being willing to ruin someone's reputation just to make yourself feel better. This is cowardly, spiteful and vengeful.

There are of course plenty more. This is only a general idea. Now let's list a few things that ARE integrity:

1. Absolute honesty.

2. A willingness to be wrong, including being proved wrong in public.

3. A willingness to being exposed. (Because you have nothing to hide.)

4. Being totally trustworthy, which means you are likely to trust others.

5. Having honour. (This does not mean stubborn pride.)

6. Having principles; definite principles.

7. Accepting full responsibility for yourself.

8. Accepting full responsibility for your words and actions (no matter who or what prompted/caused them), and the effects they have on others.

9. Feeling fully responsible for your mistakes and being willing to rectify if at all possible.

10. Being able to tell the difference between truth and noble reasons, and choosing the truth, or at least being honest about having noble reasons.

11. Keeping your word. Saying what you mean, meaning what you say and doing what you said you would.

12. Having the courage to confront in order to clear up misunderstandings or problems, and also having the consideration to remain humble or fair at the same time. Never bear grudges or brood or hate, never even telling the person you have a problem with them. Courageously telling people face to face if you have some problem with them.

13. Being willing to take a good hard look at yourself and remembering that no one in the world owes you anything, not even the person you've been married to for 30 years. Knowing that you can take care of

yourself and take care of others and insisting on fairness, equality and win/win solutions.

14. Realising that good luck or hard- earned money gained by your friends and family is theirs and you have absolutely no right to it at all, no matter what you've done for them in the past, what the history is, or who you are to them.

15. Realising that your bad luck is your bad luck, and not trying to lump the burden on to others.

16. Saying only good words about others, or keeping your negative opinions private, or refusing to comment. Only giving your personal negative opinion to people who actually ask you for your honest opinion. Never spreading gossip and your personal grievances about others to people not involved. Keeping this information privately amongst only those directly involved.

17. Always paying the fair agreed price, never bullying people into giving you more goods or a cheaper price at their expense and loss. Always paying your bills on time and being honourable with your financial commitments and promises.

Again, there are many, many more, this is only a general idea.

We can have different amounts of integrity. We can have none, a little or a whole lot. For example: you kindly lend me your car for the day. As far as you know, there is nothing wrong with the car. I'm driving along and it breaks down.

Level zero integrity: I abandon your useless piece of scrap on the side of the road. When you eventually phone to find out where your car is, I shout at you angrily telling you what hell I went through because of you.

Low level integrity: I abandon your car on the side of the road. I go in search of a telephone to tell you that your car has broken down, and it's not my fault. I'm willing to try to find someone who will tow it back to you, but can't promise.

Medium level integrity: (where most people are): I find someone to help me, and I tow the car back to you. I apologize and tell you I don't know how it happened and I hope it wasn't something I did.

Medium/high level of integrity: I find someone to help me, I tow the car back to you. I apologize and I start phoning to find out how much it will cost you to fix it. I try to find a friend who will fix it cheaply or for free. I get you the best bargain I can possibly find. I offer to contribute a bit towards the costs.

High level of integrity: By hook or by crook I get your car fixed and returned at my expense. I borrowed it and it was working when it left your house. For these two reasons, it is my responsibility to give it back in the working condition it was in when I took it. It was my bad luck that it happened to break down on me, therefore it is my unexpected expense. I tell you that the car broke down and I give you the name and phone number of the person who fixed it in case there are problems with his repair job.

Integrity is taking full responsibility for everything that happens in us and to us, without taking everything so seriously and without leaning on anyone or blaming anyone and without expecting compensation when unavoidable bad luck happens. It is peacefully accepting the inevitable and the unwanted consequences that sometimes occur while at the same time, standing tall and strong and resourceful, ready to do what is necessary to put things right. But it is more than that. It is huge courage and huge consideration. It is trusting ourselves 100% so that we are able to trust others 100%, even after some crook has done us in. It is being broad minded enough to separate one bad incident from the rest of life. One bad person from the rest of mankind. One bad deed from all other deeds in the same person.

Imagine what a wonderful world this would be to live in if everyone strived for and insisted upon integrity!

Special Thanks

One last thing before I go

When you have succeeded in your own mental combat and become victorious, you will find your children, family members and other loved ones absolutely blossom under your calm, wise guidance. Your staff or subordinates will respond well to you and perhaps even love you. You will be trusted and trustworthy. People will feel safe with you because they will be able to confide in you and tell you their truth without fear of consequences, and they'll know you are trust worthy. The increased popularity will make you feel safe, useful, loved and welcome. You will indeed find inner peace and happiness, because both are after all, only a state of mind.

Special thanks

My special and most grateful thanks to all the wise and wonderful philosophers, teachers, psychologists, psychiatrists, lecturers and personal-growth gurus and spiritual teachers out there – those who taught me and those who so kindly published all their wisdom in books, manuals, CDs, DVDs, videos and tapes, readily available for the rest of us to read and learn from. Thank you to all the people and organizations who hold so many training sessions, seminars and workshops for people to attend to learn and experience. You all saved my life, my sanity, my happiness and my children. I studied your work intensely and most of my teachings were originally derived from your wisdom. You may recognize your wisdom here and there in my book. I could not mention all of you because you are too many, but please know that I am deeply grateful, and I hope my book is a credit to everything you all have taught. Thank you to Nightingale Conant Corporation for getting so much wisdom out there for sale and the messages of the great wise ones heard.

Thank you to all the companies that employed me to teach conflict management to the staff. In the process, I learned a lot more than I taught.

Thank you to all the thousands of clients and patients I've seen over the years. The problems you brought to me to help you to solve made everything I was learning real to me, and my increasing success rate with all of you was all the proof I needed.

Thank you to all the thousands of students I've taught over the years. Your attending my trainings and workshops, bringing all your wonderful ideas with you, has taught me more than you'll know and I feel so totally honoured and grateful that you let me share this all with you. Your attendance kept me going and kept the money coming in so I could keep learning, attending courses and teaching others.

Thank you to all of you who have changed your lives around for the better as a result of the trainings because that has done much more than you can imagine towards making the world a better place for all of us to live in.

Thank you to all the trainers I've trained. You are all out there spreading the good news. Thank you to my children for bringing me up.

Thank you for my confidence.
Thank you for my hope.
Thank you for the many ways
you taught me how to cope.

Thank you for the healing
you taught me how to find,
by showing me that heroes
were only in my mind.

Thank you for the wisdom
you pressed on me to seek
For now I see my silence
no longer needs to speak.

Many are the memories
I treasure now as art,
from which I paint my future
and colourize my heart.

by Terri Ann Laws